THE GROWNUPS GUIDE TO
RUNNING AWAY FROM HOME

Earn Dollars. Spend Pesos. Escape to Paradise.

By

DIANE HUTH

The Runaway Sherpa

Published by

ISLA
Publishing Group

Isla Publishing Group

San Antonio, TX and Isla Mujeres, Mexico

Lorna -
Welcome to such a
paradise!
pleasure
to meet you!
Enjoy! Diane

PUBLISHER'S NOTE:
This publication is designed to provide accurate information at the time of publication. It is sold with the understanding that the author and publisher are not engaged in rendering legal, financial, accounting, medical or other professional services. If you require legal advice or expert assistance, you should seek the services of a competent professional.

Any brand names or logos are used in an editorial fashion, and the author and publisher claim no relationship with or ownership of other companies other than specifically noted herein.

Any recommendations for action, vendors or service providers are the sole opinion of the author.

All stories about individuals in this book are true, and the individuals have either agreed to have their first name and story shared, or have requested that the author change their name and some details to protect their privacy. But the people are real, and so are their stories.

Published by

San Antonio, TX USA

DEDICATION

My mother and father were adventurers in their youth. During World War II, they moved from Minnesota to Canada to work in a war munitions factory.

During the early 1950s, they left their auto sales and service business in frozen Minnesota in good hands of a mechanic and tow truck operator, and spent two months every winter exploring old-world Mexico by car – very adventuresome more than 70 years ago.

Later in the 1950s, they sold the car dealership and ran away from home permanently, moving their young family more than 1,700 miles south to a white sandy beach in sunny Southwest Florida.

I grew up on that magical silky white sand beach, dashing out the door to plunge into the bathtub-warm turquoise surf, and I felt that I was in paradise.

As my parents grew older, they, like most of us, became burdened with the responsibilities of life, and traveled less and less. We did a family vacation in Europe for a month in the 1970s, and they visited me as I moved to live in Spain, Brazil and Mexico City. But they lost their sense of adventure, and stayed close to home, abandoning the discovery of new foreign locales.

But they passed on to me their early sense of adventure, and I studied Spanish in Madrid, Spain in the '70s, which led me to a life of exploration living and working overseas. But like them, as the years passed, my world of adventure shrunk to encompass work and family responsibilities, relieved by occasional week-long vacations to a tropic beach somewhere beautiful.

Somehow, as we age, we forget about pure unbridled joy and freedom, and accept the yoke of responsibility instead. We build a life living in four climate-controlled walls, and fill our days, months, and years with the minutia of life in America.

But it doesn't have to be that way.

As we age, we can regain – or claim for the first time – that sense of awe and adventure that we enjoyed in our youth.

I was able to escape at the last minute, as I was being crushed by the burden of responsibility, and I ran away to paradise to find the joy and fulfillment I had been missing in my life for a very long time.

And so can you.

I wrote this book to show you the way to reinvent your life, to cast off the fear of the unknown, to break free from the daily mind-numbing routine of life, and to seize a life of wonder, adventure, joy and gratitude for being at the right place at the right time in your life.

It's a lesson I learned from my mother and father, who blazed the way more than seven decades ago.

And as I embark on daily new experiences in my wonderful life in paradise, I envision their spirits perched on my left shoulder, savoring my life of adventure, and ecstatic for me that I was able to follow in their footsteps and find my life of joy in paradise.

Thanks, Mom and Dad. I made it, with your help.

HERE'S A VALUABLE
FREE GIFT FOR YOU

———

Throughout this book, I refer you to my website www.GrownUpsGuide.com, where I bring you a wealth of information, resources, and links.

There is just too much information that can change on a daily basis to try to document it in this book, as it could become out of date at any time.

So I encourage you to visit my website often, to access more than six valuable free gifts that can help you on your journey to escape to paradise.

Here is one of them: Your Ultimate Immigration Guide To Mexico.

I walk you step-by-step through everything you need to understand the often-confusing rules and regulations of Mexican Immigration.

And I will keep it updated when the rules change – as they will probably do often!

So download it now to get yourself started on your journey to paradise.

Download it now at www.YourImmigrationGuideToMexico.com.

And enjoy your journey to find and escape to paradise – faster and easier than you ever dreamed possible!

Diane Huth

The Runaway Sherpa

ACKNOWLEGMENTS

So many people have helped me on my journey of discovery which prompted the creation of this book, that it will be impossible to acknowledge them all, but I will try.

It always starts with family:

Of course, my family members have been an inspiration, especially my mom and dad, **Helen and Gordon Clauss,** who ran away from home in Minnesota to spend two months every winter exploring colonial Mexico back in the 1950s.

I took my love for adventure from them, as did my brother **Gordon Clauss,** who fell in love first with rural France, and then lost his heart to the beauty of Croatia. His mission to save the world's bee population by the invention and manufacture of various non-chemical products to improve the health of bee colonies has been slowed down by a recent heart attack and stroke, and I am praying for his full recovery so he can continue with his life's work which impacts us all. And I really appreciate the untiring efforts of his wife **Lois Laseur** who has cared for him throughout this challenging time.

I hope I have instilled the passion for adventure into my precious son **Alex Huth,** so he and his wife **Rachel Coy Huth** can continue their world travels despite the upcoming birth of my first grandbaby, currently called **Blueberry** in lieu of a gender-specific name awaiting the outcome of the birth. Somehow, I feel that nickname will carry on, much to the chagrin of the child who will be stuck with it in the future.

My cousins, aunts and uncles, and nieces and nephews are a source of joy, and I thank you for your love and support. Special thanks go out to **Debbie, Lenny, Nathan and Lea Tropiano** for your frequent visits to San Antonio, and taking on the responsibility of distributing the memoirs of my family's life after I flew to paradise.

And my cousin **Sara Keyes** made my move so much more exciting by visiting just four days after I arrived in paradise, giving me a reason to explore and experience so many wonderful places together.

<u>Friends were critical in my journey to paradise:</u>

I want to thank my many friends in San Antonio and around the world who have supported me in this journey. You are too many to name fully, but please know that I appreciate your support and friendship.

When I needed a word of encouragement, or someone to rush over the night before the estate sale to take home freezers full of food, or sit with my mom when I had to run out to work or an emergency, you were there for me, and still are. **Jackie, Marie, Kathy, Kay, JoAnne, Beth, Sue, Mickie, Gina, Emma, Elizabeth, Ray, John, Lyndie,** and all my other friends – thank you for being there at my side or on the phone to offer a word of encouragement and support.

Marie Ferrante helped me pack my belongings, get rid of lots of unwanted stuff, forced me to make painful decisions, and relieved me of many responsibilities as I prepared for first an estate sale, and then a final move out in preparation for departing to paradise.

Melissa May and **Javier Martinez** babysat my dog Teddy for a month before he could join me in paradise, and they were great foster parents. Teddy didn't always behave, and sat by the front door for two days after I dropped him off, but they wooed him with love and attention and lots of treats and walks – thanks so much. They enjoyed it so much they adopted their own puppy, and are smitten with him, so it was a happy ending for everyone involved.

Jackie Perry helped care for my mom for many months, especially when I was traveling, and offered me a room in her home to store my treasures. She flew down to paradise to visit and bring my dog Teddy, planning to stay a week, and stayed for two months instead. During that time, we had many wonderful adventures and some unpleasant landlord issues, and it was great to have her there to help me through it all.

Likewise, **Sue Arent** came for a one-day visit, and stayed for a month, and I loved every minute of it. I learned so much from her old soul spiritual wisdom as we celebrated life on this magical Island of Women, which was the sacred healing sanctuary of the principal Mayan Goddess Ixchel.

Maureen Rojas visited me twice with her son **Charlie,** and I got to be Auntie Adventure to encourage him to embrace new experiences.

Visits from dear friends are especially welcome, and I treasure the time we spend together.

Many true friends helped me care for my mom:

For more than five years, I cared for my mom as she withered away from the terrible disease of dementia, and I have deep gratitude for the support of the many wonderful people who helped me in that difficult labor of love.

David Jensen was with me for almost two decades and committed to help care for her until she passed on, despite the terrible wear and tear on his life and mine.

Marie Ferrante sat with her when I had to be away, patiently putting up with the constantly repeated questions without answers, and encouraging me to take better care of myself in light of the oppressing burden of care I felt I had to provide.

Maricela Azuara provided wonderful loving care of my mom when she no longer knew who I was and cherished her and attended to her every need lovingly and patiently. I can't say enough to thank her for her care and recommend her **Amazing Hands Private Care Home** to anyone looking for an excellent home to care for an ill loved one. Having such a loving team to care for her in her dementia-ravaged state allowed me to escape to paradise, where I was finally able to care for myself and recapture the joy I'd lost years before in the burden of family responsibility.

Brook Carey and **Bob Bueker** hosted me for two different respite trips to their amazingly beautiful time share condo in Puerto Vallarta, where I was able to shed the yoke of responsibility and sleep and recharge from the burden of caregiving.

<u>I am so grateful to all my new friends here in paradise:</u>

I am incredibly blessed to have bonded with so many wonderful people here in Isla Mujeres, the paradise that I call home, and it is impossible to mention them all. I have told you about many of them throughout the book, although with first names only, but they know who they are. I can only mention five, or it could take up the whole book if I got carried away.

At my very first Sisters of Perpetual Disorder coffee in July 2019, I met two women who have become my very closest friends here in Isla.

Dawn Fleming and I instantly bonded when we discovered that we are fellow Funnel Hackers (which means we use the same funnel building software ClickFunnels – what a coincidence!) We are both on a mission to help others redesign their lives by moving overseas, offering similar products and services to different target customers. We share both personal and business affinities, and it is great to have a brilliant businesswomen friend to toss ideas around with, and to ask questions and seek and receive support.

Helena Gebrier is a French native and long-time Isla resident, and we quickly became fast friends. She hosted me to a farewell dinner at a lovely restaurant on Hidalgo, the walking street, at the end of my Beta Test, and welcomed me back to the island with a delightful lunch when I moved back two months later. Whenever I need a contact or referral, she is the one who knows the answer. When my precious dog Buddy died of old age in his sleep, she came right over to comfort me. She arranged for a friend to dig a grave for him on a piece of windswept land and helped me wrap his body in a colorful wrap and adorn it with ribbons and beads and drove me to the burial site. This is a true friend, and I am blessed to have her here in my life.

Zoila and Rogelio Chuc are my next-door neighbors and are a delightful couple who have become dear friends and loyal supporters. They have keys to my house and car, and I know I can trust them to look out for my interests and make sure I am okay. I tell you about them in the book, but I want to acknowledge them here as well. Whenever I have a question about local culture, they provide the answer, and help me understand why things are the way they are. It's a two-way street, and I help them as much as they help me – but that's what friendship is all about, isn't it?

Of course, I have to acknowledge my landlord, **Jorge Antonio Dzul**, a young man who has built the lovely house I call my home, and lives next door in much more modest accommodations. He has treated me wonderfully and has made living here in paradise easier and hassle-free. He and his whole family look out for my best interests, make sure I have a parking place, invite me to birthday parties and family events, provide upgrades or modifications I request, and come running to immediately fix any issue I have with the house. If every landlord were so kind and considerate, there would be no landlord tenant problems in the world.

And lastly, I want to acknowledge the **wonderful people of Mexico and particularly Isla Mujeres,** who welcome me into their country, town and lives. I am stimulated every day by the amazing history and culture I learn and observe, and I feel blessed to live here among you. Thank you for your hospitality and grace.

The Resources That Helped Me Move To Paradise

I read and researched a lot before I embarked on my trip to paradise, and I had several mentors along the way – whether they knew it or not.

In 2007, **Tim Ferris** rocked the world with his best-selling book **The Four Hour Work Week,** which my son Alex gifted to workaholic me to help me learn to work less. He came up with the term geoarbitrage to explain the benefit of moving to a low-cost market to leverage your scarce resources. He pioneered the concept of the digital nomad years before the technology became available to build a remote lifestyle. He showed us how to create online income, leverage offshore talent and Virtual Assistants, and build automated systems we today call marketing automation. I'd like to consider myself to be the Tim Ferris for Retirement Age Women – blazing the way for my generation to reinvent their lives overseas. it has a ring to it, doesn't it?

Robert Kiyosaki changed the world in 1997 with his blockbuster book **Rich Dad, Poor Dad.** He explained our misconception about money, and helped people understand that assets are things that make you money, and liabilities are things that cost you money – like your house and car. He created the foundation for the financial principals we discuss in this book, and provided a different perspective to financial management that transformed the world.

Jackie Flynn is the publisher of **International Living Magazine,** which was instrumental in opening my mind to the idea of moving to paradise. I read it faithfully for two years, learning from the articles, and visualizing myself in the runaway lifestyle before I had the nerve to reach for it myself.

And **Winton Churchill** is the Founder of **Barefoot Consultants** and has created a business showing people how to find work that will support their lifestyle in paradise.

This book didn't happen without the help of my writing and publishing coaches:

Lots of people can write a book, but writing a book that sells requires skill and knowledge, so I sought help and coaching from various experts:

I learned a lot about book content creation from **Nicholas Boothman** and **Ken Dunn**, both New York Times best-selling authors and writing and speaking coaches.

And I was able to bring this book to final completion with the coaching of **Raymond Aaron**, NY Times bestselling author of two business books, two Chicken Soup for the Soul books, a Dummies book, and more than 140 books he has cowritten with other authors. He taught me how to structure the book format for commercial success, and showed me how to quickly create the content to be able to write a book in a clear system that ensures success.

And **Naval Kumar** was the Book Architect working with Raymond Aaron who helped me edit and refine my content, and put it in a commercial platform to generate sales quickly.

To all four gentlemen, thanks so much for what you have taught me that has resulted in this book in this format. I hope I did you proud.

My partner and greatest fan is instrumental to my success and wellbeing:

During the process of writing this book, I met a wonderful man named Paul Doane who has grounded me in life, and nurtures and protects me, and often nudges me to improvement when needed. I don't want to give away too much, as I tell you about him in the last chapter, but to Paul, I send you my love and thanks.

WHY I WROTE THIS BOOK

I'm Diane Huth, The Runaway Sherpa, and I want to help you learn how easy it is to live a life of joy and freedom in paradise for a fraction of what you're paying right now.

I ran away from home in 2019, and never looked back. I left my job as a university professor of marketing and homebound caregiver to my elderly mom with dementia, and landed on a tropical island that is as close to heaven as you can imagine.

When I tell people I meet that I live here full time, they want to know HOW?

So I have written for you the definitive guide freedom-seekers need: **The GrownUps Guide To Running Away From Home – Earn Dollars, Spend Pesos, Escape to Paradise**.

It chronicles my journey to move to the tiny island of Isla Mujeres off the coast of Cancun in Mexico, while working remotely as an author, career coach, and marketing consultant.

I have realized that working inside during the day is a waste of sunbeams, and I will help freedom lovers like you discover how to escape drudgery and routine to live the life you have always yearned for. Plus, to finance your plan to run away from home, I will introduce you to many different ways to create a remote income deposited in dollars into your bank account back home.

In this book, I share all my tips, insight, experiences (good and bad) and strategies for success with you – so you too can escape to paradise today!

I look forward to holding your hand and guiding you on your exciting journey to the life you always dreamed of.

Diane Huth

The Runaway Sherpa

TABLE OF CONTENTS

PROLOGUE – A SNAPSHOT OF MY NEW LIFE IN PARADISE

———

July 2019

Today was a typical day in paradise.

I slept in until about 9:30 a.m., nestled in my soundproof cocoon of cement block walls and a tall cement outer wall surrounding the six-unit condo, now empty except for me during the doldrums of the summer "low season". and the small pool which is my front yard.

I lay in bed for half an hour, checking messages and emails on my phone before deciding what to do today.

I responded to potential coaching clients who wanted to schedule an appointment, dictating responses while lying in my cloud-like king bed.

I slipped on a long flowered stretchy dress au natural, before sauntering into the kitchen, and filled my thermal mug with sparking mineral water, ice, and half a shiny green lime. So refreshing!

Before running away from home, I used to drag myself out of bed, and stumble to the kitchen where I slugged down two or three cups of coffee before coming awake enough to function. Here, I don't need or miss the caffeine at all, and savor the cool crisp sparking water instead. And I don't set an alarm clock, letting my circadian rhythms tell my body when to wake up refreshed and relaxed.

I skipped breakfast as I always do now, conscious of my hours of intermittent fasting, which feels incredibly good as well as doing great things for my health and weight. Instead, I put on my baggy "at home" swimsuit and jumped in the tiny condo pool located just out the front door for a leisurely 20-minute swim.

When I got out, I sat on the patio and made phone calls to catch up with friends, handled routine business, and took care of some issues in caring for my elderly mom in a nursing home. I talked to a couple of prospective clients and texted others with my available hours for the day.

Dried off enough not to get chilled when stepping back into the air conditioning, I slipped back into my bold floral dress, and sat down at the computer for write a resume for my newest career coaching client.

Two hours later, I emailed of the first draft of the resume, and went to the kitchen to make ceviche for lunch. I removed a package from the refrigerator containing a small fillet of some kind of white fish and diced it into ½" tidbits. I squeezed the juice of four large limes into the bowl of fish and set it aside to marinate for half an hour until the lime juice "cooked" the fish flakes into a firm opaque white delicacy.

I finely diced a small red onion, two small Roma tomatoes, and lots of cilantro leaves and stems, adding and stirring them into the white flaky fish. I added generous amounts of salt and black pepper, and then thinly sliced and diced avocado, and by the time I was done, it was ready to enjoy. I savored a quiet late lunch of the ceviche with crackers while listening to music from Pandora, and then decided to run out to introduce myself to my soon-to-be new dentist, whom I saw on Facebook had office hours today.

I threw on another shorter stretchy dress over a different dry and not so ratty swimsuit, and hopped in my tiny, rented Volkswagen Gol to drive the two miles to the dentist, learning new streets along the way.

After a brief yet very pleasant conversation with the well-recommended dentist, Doctora Victoria, who was alone in her little walk up one room office, I decided to explore a new beach on the Caribbean side of the island. I drove the couple of blocks to the ocean, then drove to the south end of the island, looking for cars parked alongside the road and people in the surf. I found a spot with a small white sandy beach at the bottom of a short path down through windswept rocks and walked carefully down to the nearly abandoned shore. I collected some tiny seashells and sea glass and walked out past waist height in the shallow water with brisk waves coming in from the direction of Cuba. There was one Mexican man in the water, with his two teen sons lounging on the waterline, so I was alone yet not at risk of being swept away to sea.

After half an hour of bobbing like a champagne cork in the bathtub warm aquamarine water, I drove to Chedraui, the largest supermarket on the island, to get cash from the ATM machine, and bought some bottles of mineral water.

By then it was after 4:00, and I headed to the south side of the tiny four-mile-long island, to the bay side facing Cancun just 8 miles west across deep turquoise water, for my late afternoon swim at Capitan Dulche's Beach Club. I am a "regular" there, ordering my single can of sparkling water for $3 (no cover charge, so I don't mind the pricy beverage), and taking a long, luxurious swim in the gorgeous semi-saltwater pool attached to the beautifully decorated outdoor cabana restaurant and bar.

I shared the bathtub-temperature pool with some kids I had met there the previous week and was greeted by their mom who recognized me from prior encounters. We chatted, and talked about common friends in San Antonio, where we both came from. She and her husband own a large chain of quesadilla restaurants in Mexico and are expanding to the US. When I introduced myself as a marketing and branding consultant and career coach, she invited me to visit her Cancun restaurant and meet with them to see if I could help them with marketing and franchising their business in the US. That's how business is done here in Mexico, with people you know and have recommendations about, traveling in the same socio-economic circles.

After drying off, I rested on the luxurious bed-like lounge beside the beach until the sun set, checking emails and reading a book, and I was one of the last guests to leave, as always. What a wonderful and restful afternoon!

I was really hungry by that time, since I had only eaten fish ceviche for lunch, and decided to go to my favorite expatriate hang out, The Soggy Peso. It's a small luxury hotel or guesthouse, built by a retired couple from Dallas, Mal and Sally, who occupy the top floor of the beautifully decorated property, which includes four guest suites, a small pool draped with flowers and greenery, a tiny popular beach bar and a great little outdoor eatery. The food is cooked fresh to order from a limited menu and served by the bar staff who have worked there for more than six years, thankful for a great job with great tips from the American patrons. I talked with several people I knew and got a referral for a carpenter who can make frames to stretch an art canvas that I brought from the States. I also chatted with a man who is putting together a consortium to deal with the Sargasso Sea grass epidemic that is seriously impacting other beaches, but thankfully not my beautiful Island, and I was pleased to learn so much about the issue and possible remedies. I enjoyed a delicious beef taco plate, and then headed home to crank up the computer and go to work for the rest of the evening.

I've been typing since about 9 p.m., and it's now nearly 2 a.m., so I've been able to put in my seven or eight hours of work today, while still enjoying the beautiful day outside. I've realized that daylight hours are absolutely wasted by working inside in an office! I've always been a night owl, so I love quiet late nights where I can work undisturbed and get into my ultra-productive and creative "zone." I have evolved my schedule through trial and error to find the way to best combine my need to work for a living, with my desire to savor every minute of paradise in the sunshine and inviting ocean and pool water. I have even written down and posted my "Work Hours" on the refrigerator to help me keep on schedule.

I will finish this chapter, and call it a night, heading to bed without setting the alarm. Then tomorrow, I will start on another beautiful day in paradise.

. . . .

Would you like to spend your days like this?

If so, this book is for you. You too can live a life of joy in paradise. Keep reading to learn how it is easier and less scary than you ever imagined possible.

1. DO YOU YEARN TO LIVE A LIFE OF JOY IN PARADISE?

If this sounds like what your heart has been aching for, read on.

I will share with you my journey from burnt out overworked homebound caregiver to a free and happy "escapee", living the life I've always dreamed of.

I will also provide you with a road map to escape your current life and learn how to successfully run away, whether you are 30 or 70.

And I'll share ways to live richly on as little as your monthly Social Security check alone.

If you are well off financially, such a move is easy.

And if you are struggling to survive on a shoestring budget, you can actually live a life of joy and fulfillment in a place that makes your heart beat faster.

While I will share my journey to Isla Mujeres, my white sandy beach in Mexico, it's definitely not the only way to achieve freedom. But this is where my heart sings.

Your "happy place" may be a cabin in the mountains, a loft in a big city, a sun-kissed house in a colonial village, or a small yacht sailing anywhere you want. The process of running away from home to gain personal, economic and spiritual freedom is the same, regardless of the destination you choose.

And if you choose to move to Mexico, the #1 retirement destination for Americans, where more than one million US citizens choose to call home, I will hold you by the hand to teach you the insiders' secrets to a successful transition.

And I'll show you how you can supplement your fixed income with work that allows you to earn dollars, spend pesos, and live in paradise!

Come along and join me in my journey to freedom and joy. I'll show you the way, so you can fearlessly and confidently embark on your own journey of adventure and liberation.

2. WHY I DECIDED TO RUN AWAY FROM HOME

Life Happens

L ife happens, and at some point, you look around and wonder, "Where have all the years gone?"

I had my only son, Alex, late in life, at age 38. Before he was born, I enjoyed a wonderful international career in marketing, working for premier companies Johnson & Johnson in Brazil and Portugal, and Frito-Lay in Mexico in the early 1980s. My career in marketing and brand management took me to Los Angeles, Miami and then San Antonio. I was blessed to work with great companies – including Mission Foods, RJ Reynolds, Carnation/Nestle, and CBS Cable TV.

I enjoyed a great salary, earning six figures, serving as VP of Marketing, and winning sales junkets to exotic locations. I loved my career in Corporate America – and I was good at it. And yes, I was a workaholic, but that's what it took to be successful in business, especially as a woman.

Over the past 15 years, I partnered in several startups, investing both time and money, and ours were some of the 90% that didn't make it for one reason or the other. One was wiped out in the dotcom crash of 2001. Another couldn't get startup funding. A third died when our key investor and technology partner had a change of management, and the new CEO cancelled the program his first day in the office.

The last straw was Biovideo – a wonderful startup gifting breathtakingly beautiful maternity videos to new parents. But the business model was flawed, based on inaccurate assumptions by the CEO, and we couldn't make the business work. The company has been hanging on by its teeth for years, struggling to find the optimal business model, unable to pay me my previous six figure salary. I continued to work for several years with no salary waiting for the turnaround that never happened.

I invested more than half of my 401K buying equity in the company in the heady early days of the venture. As the corporate treasurer, I signed the applications for the corporate credit cards, not realizing that I was also signing as a guarantor! Later as the challenges grew and the other investors bailed, I financed short-term working capital with my personal credit cards. It was never intentional, just answering urgent needs: "We need $3,000 to make payroll." "We need $5,000 for sales tax or they will close us down. " "The hurricane damaged our computers and cameras, and insurance won't pay for it, so we need to buy $2,500 of equipment so our employees can go to work on Monday." And it was always a short-term loan – I would get it back next week, next month. But I never did, because there was always the next dire disaster breathing down our necks.

I am now out more than $400,000 of investment capital and direct cash loans to the company and stuck paying off about $35,000 of company debt that's racking up 24% interest each year. Ouch. I have to take responsibility for bad decisions I've made, and then figure out how to work my way out of the mess.

I was too loyal. I stayed too long because I really believed in our mission. And at first, I could justify the additional investment as I was earning six figures. Then they couldn't pay my full salary, so I agreed to continue to work full time, but for half pay. And then I agreed to drop my pay by half once again – to just a quarter of my prior salary – just enough to pay the immediate bills. Then the day came that we had to make a terrible choice. There were two senior executives, me and the COO, and one of us had to go. We could only afford one salary. And I couldn't do what he did, so I offered to leave.

I thought I could get another job.

Foolish me.

I Needed a New Job – Fast

I needed money. I was tapped out. My 401K was down to just one quarter of what it was when I started. And my million dollars of equity in the business was gone with the wind.

I'd invested it in the business, and then in living expenses while not getting paid for several years.

But I was 65 years old, and I soon discovered that no one would hire me in corporate America. I couldn't even get through the door to submit my application, much less get an interview. AT&T had their global headquarters in San Antonio where I lived, and they advertised 19 marketing positions that I was extremely qualified for. I applied for them repeatedly over a period of a year, and never even got an acknowledgement from them, much less an interview or a job. I even went down to the corporate headquarters recruiting office, and tried to hand deliver my resume to HR, and they refused to take it! They turned me away in the lobby and told me to apply online – like I had been doing for a year!

I Needed More Than Just Money

I needed money, but just as importantly - I needed to feel valued, relevant, important, needed. My career had been so important to me all those years. I defined myself by my career. Without a career, who was I? I was lost.

I couldn't get in the door for a corporate job. I was just too old to even be considered for a position I had rocked 20 years before. Panicked, I decided I could teach marketing at a university, anything to bring in some extra cash. I've got two master's degrees and a stellar corporate marketing background, right? So I applied to five different universities - and I was stunned when three of them hired me the same week - teaching three different classes, using three different text books, and three different learning management programs and software, three different days a week. The learning curve almost killed me. But I struggled through, learned the systems, survived, and each semester was a bit easier. And I was making enough to barely survive.

Teaching as an adjunct professor pays a pittance. But it gave me lots of prestige and launched me on my career as an author.

I was teaching marketing and branding, so when I discovered that my bright talented students didn't know how to write a resume or create a LinkedIn page, I prepared a presentation to teach them how to use the marketing skills I teach them in class to market themselves. The presentation grew up to become a lecture, seminar, and then a book. It's called **BRAND YOU! To Land Your Dream Job** and it's an Amazon best seller. I promoted my book at national conferences and invested tens of thousands of dollars in professional development and resources to learn to market my book in the ultra-competitive publishing industry. But it never made it to the big leagues, as a self-published book sold through Amazon and other online retailers doesn't command any kind of retail presence, publisher publicity, or promotion programs.

I Wasn't Alone in the Unemployment Crisis

Then I discovered that my mature professional peers – people that I know, have worked with, and esteem – are facing terrible age

11

discrimination, and unable to find work in their 50s and 60s. No one will hire "seasoned" workers who are seen as "overqualified" – meaning too old or too expensive. So I wrote my next book **REINVENT YOUR CAREER – Beat Age Discrimination to Land Your Dream Job** to help my generation learn how to keep or find employment as long as possible in this youth-focused employment environment. This book got a lot of interest from radio and podcast hosts, and I have done more than 150 media interviews. But that still doesn't sell enough books to pay for my website hosting.

I worked hard to learn how to become a successful author. I hired writing and promotion coaches, subscribed to educational programs, bought databases of journalists and libraries, traveled to New York to promote my books to more than 140 leading journalists and radio and TV producers – twice!

$80K later, further draining my 401K, I've appeared on more than 150 radio shows, podcasts, and TV shows, as a guest speaker talking about careers. I ranked high in Google searches. I have 100,000 followers on Facebook. But I wasn't selling very many books! I was making between $200 and $300 each month on book royalties – which wasn't enough to pay even the electric bill. And I was spending more than $1,500 a month in social media, virtual assistants, graphic designers, content creation, website hosting and development. Something had to change, but I didn't know what or how.

Still, with my teaching salary and Social Security I was managing to scratch out a living, with the help of some money from my 401K. I was supporting a home for myself, my elderly mom, and my longtime partner, David, who helped me with home responsibilities, but never contributed financially. But I wasn't living…I was just existing. I longed to escape – to run away from home and responsibilities. To be free. Every time I went on vacation, it was to a white sandy beach somewhere tropical, and I said, "As soon as I can, I want to live here."

I hungered for it. I needed it. But I was trapped – both financially and by family responsibilities.

Caring for My Mom Almost Killed Me

My mom moved in with me more than 25 years ago, when my dad died and I got divorced, helping to care for my then 5-year-old son. And we lived together and moved together ever since, and I've been blessed to have her at my side and watching my back and giving me a helping hand all my life. She was my best friend, my biggest supporter, my confidant, the person I could rely on for anything. But then she was struck with dementia, and her brain withered, and I helplessly watched her devolve from the brilliant woman I knew and loved to a small child, and then even worse. Her mental facilities deteriorated day by day. First she forgot how to play cards, then large jigsaw puzzles, finally simple eight-piece puzzles. Her decline continued to the point that she couldn't talk and make sense, didn't know where she was, couldn't hold a conversation, watch a TV show, or express anything other than basic physical needs. She became incontinent, wheelchair bound, and looked at me with pale empty eyes as she poured her coffee out on the floor or refused to eat, then forgot how to swallow food. She constantly asked, "Where am I?" and "Who are you?" When she asked me if I was her mother, or said she wanted to go home, it broke my heart and wounded my soul.

Wheelchair bound, incontinent, unable to stand or utter a coherent sentence, she was beyond my ability to care for her, even with three weekly hospice visits, and the valiant help of David, my partner of 19 years. He was a saint and promised to stay with me and help me care for her until she passed. But this was worse than death. I prayed every day that she would have an aneurism in her sleep, smiling as she joins all her other family members. Because at age 97, anything that can happened to her would be worse – pneumonia, Covid, a stroke, cancer, heart attack, broken hip, you name it.

Caring for her was a full-time job, and I felt trapped and imprisoned in my own home. I had to schedule time to go to teach, go to the doctor, or leave the house, because like a two-year-old, she couldn't be left alone for a minute. The thought of popping out to have a glass of wine with a girlfriend or going out to a movie was just not feasible. And she was too heavy and unwieldly to easily take out, even for special occasions or a doctor's visit.

And like a two-year-old, she wanted attention. She was not happy sitting in her wheelchair next to my desk while I worked. She couldn't watch TV or read a book or carry on a conversation. It must have been hell for her, trapped in a mind that didn't work anymore. And it was hell for me and everyone else who cared for her and remembered the brilliant woman she was just a few years ago.

At some point in this process, I realized I couldn't care for her anymore - and that it didn't matter to her since she didn't know who I was any more.

Throughout this long difficult process, I'd been fantasizing about running away from home – and from all that. But I also want to run TO something good – joy, fulfillment, adventure, freedom, and more.

And as I got older, I had a sense of my time running out as well. I've seen what 85 and 90 looks like, and I don't like it. I had a palpable sense of urgency to get out and become alive again.

But I was stuck working and writing, trying to make a living - and I felt like I was dying. I was 80+ pounds overweight, wore 2XX clothes, hated the way I looked, and I felt even worse. I was always exhausted, never got enough sleep, and needed two cups of heavily sweetened coffee just to function in the morning. I was a prisoner of my own home, trapped in the routine of working, then caring for my mom around the clock. Hospice care helped, but as she declined, so did I. I was crushed.

This burden of responsibility finally destroyed my relationship with David. It withered away due to lack of intimacy, being trapped in the burden of responsibility of around-the-clock care, changing diapers, wiping up food thrown on the floor, relentless questions without answers, and the wrenching sorrow and feeling of guilt for not being able to fix it. As I watched my mom drift away to become a pitiful vegetable, I threw myself into work to try and fix my financial crisis. David chose alcohol to ease his pain.

I Was Trapped – and I Didn't Know How to Escape

I didn't know what to do. I had used my mom's meager Social Security and Veterans Death benefits to help pay for a comfortable handicap-equipped three-bedroom house to care for her, for medical expenses, nursing care, diapers, sitters when I had to leave, and so much more. I was trapped. I couldn't afford to put her in a nursing home, because then her income would go to the nursing home, and I would have to supplement that by another $1,000 or more a month. I would have to move to a tiny apartment which I might not be able to afford. I was earning Social Security, a pittance for teaching at just one university by that time - and I was struggling to pay off the $35,000 of company debts from Biovideo – which was costing me $1,000 a month. I didn't know what to do. My 401K was gutted, and I was taking money out every month to pay the bills. I couldn't get a professional level job in my field because of my age, and my writing career was satisfying, but definitely not making a profit. It was a net drain of at least $2,000 or more a month. So I was trapped - financially and emotionally.

I ran budget scenarios, tried to reduce expenses, tried to figure out how I could rent an apartment in San Antonio, which is a low-cost market, pay all the bills - and have anything left over. It would be tight. My Social Security was too much to get a subsidized apartment or food stamps. Perhaps I could get a small apartment in a not-so-great neighborhood, perhaps no cable TV, no luxuries. How would I live in genteel poverty?

I closed my eyes late at night and fantasized about living a life of joy on a white sandy beach where my heat would sing.

But what could I do?

I desperately wanted a better solution but didn't know how to find it.

3. FINDING JOY IN PARADISE

When I was five years old, my family moved from cold snowy Minnesota to live on Fort Myers Beach on the southwest Gulf Coast of Florida. As a small child, I ran out the door onto the brilliant white sand of the beach just steps outside our home. Joyful childhood memories for me include white sandy beaches, warm water, waves caressing the beach., the sigh of palm fronts rubbing against each other. I hate cold weather and love the sunshine.

In recent years, I spent any free time I could get away on a double wide lounge chair in the back yard, soaking up sunbeams, reading a book or sleeping a deep restful sleep in my "happy place." I laughed and told people "I'm solar powered." I closed my eyes and pretended I was at the beach.

Any vacation I was able to go on always featured a beach: Florida, Hawaii, Mexico, Puerto Rico. You name it; I'd go if it had a beach there.

About six years ago, a business acquaintance first told me about Isla Mujeres. She explained that she and her husband would spend two weeks at Thanksgiving every year on this tiny island lying seven miles east of Cancun – the most easterly place in Mexico. It's where Mexico welcomes the New Year each year, as the sun touches there first each day. She explained that she and her husband go alone for the first week, and then the kids join them the second week. She described white sandy beaches, palm trees, golf carts on the roads instead of cars, gorgeous ocean views, crashing waves on the Caribbean side and serene white beaches on the Cancun side, and I was sold.

I booked a two-week trip for myself and my mom, wheelchair bound at that time, to spend Christmas and New Year's Eve on Isla. For me, it was love at first sight. I walked off the ferry, and my heart sang with joy. My soul was at peace. And I started dreaming about living there way back then.

Then 18 months later, my girlfriend Maureen joined me on an escape vacation, and we spent a week on Isla. It was fabulous. Again, my heart sang. And Maureen relished the weeks' vacation from caring for her disabled mom and her six-year-old son as a single mom, and a high stress job as a nursing supervisor at a government-run hospital on an Indian reservation with a two-hour commute each way.

But after just a few short days, we both had to go back to reality.

Then the following year, we went back to Isla together, another great week-long escape from the realities of life, this time with her seven-year-old son Charlie. I kept talking about moving to Isla when my mom passed.

Two years later, in January, I brought my long-term partner David to Isla for 10 days. He got out early every morning, walked all over the old downtown area, called "Centro." He enjoyed it, kind of, but said he would prefer to be back in San Antonio. He'd rather watch sports on TV rather than hang out at the beach or pool. He's happy in his small apartment in a senior community and wanted to be near his doctors. He's bogged down by the stuff of life, sorting through a huge storage unit of old junk and family memories when he gets the energy to tackle the challenge. He thought I'd be bored silly here. Evidently, the beach doesn't sing to him like it does to me.

So I didn't have a partner and best friend to join me on my journey of rediscovery, and had to do it alone, which was scary. But not as terrifying as staying trapped in my home in a never-ending spiral of working, feeding and caring for my mom, trying to grab an hour of peace and quiet to read an escape novel, watching 24-hour news networks, and collapsing into bed to start all over again the next day. Giving up my dreams of freedom was much more terrifying.

My Epiphany

It was May, the end of the school year and the last teaching check for four months. As I contemplated my teaching schedule for the fall, I felt desperate. It would be another year of this, the steady decline, the desolation, the loneliness. And I thought back to my last several vacations, on a tiny island in the Caribbean. Mexico is very cheap to live in. I figured it was half the cost of living in San Antonio – or less. Food was less, utilities were less, labor a fraction of the cost in the US. On a tiny budget, I could eat out better than the drive-through junk food I ate in San Antonio. I could actually get a weekly massage for $25! And I found out I could get a decent apartment for as low as $400 or $600 a month.

I wondered – can I do it? For years I've been saying "When my mom passes, I will move to Isla Mujeres in a flash." But my mom didn't die; she just hung on in a vegetative state, in a sad world of her own, inside a mind that didn't work anymore. Could I run away to this sun-kissed white sandy beach and live in warm tropical breezes? Could I work from there – do my writing, and build my career coaching and resume writing business? Could I possibly escape to paradise?

As I looked at the impending summer and then the looming academic calendar year, I knew I had to try it right then, and not wait another year – or two – or more. The way I looked and felt I didn't know if I could survive another year or two.

My Beta Test

I looked at my frequent flier miles and discovered that I had enough Southwest Frequent Flier points to buy one ticket to Cancun, and five return tickers, each a week apart, in case there was a problem with my mom that required me to rush home. Southwest is my forever favorite airline, and they allow me to cancel any flight without penalty, returning the points to my account, so I kept cancelling upcoming return flights to extend my trial run until the last moment.

I booked the first night in a modest hotel I had stayed in on vacation and set off for a 5-week "Beta Test" or trial run to see if this was a pipe dream, or something I could really do – and enjoy.

Before I left, I diligently researched all the Facebook pages – almost a dozen for local residents and tourists. I contacted people I had met on prior trips and introduced myself to people I didn't know. My Beta Test trip was in June, which was the low season, so I was able to find a very comfortable condo with a pool for just $1,000 a month - and I took it, wiring the money by PayPal. I rented a tiny car for just $15 a day, including insurance, and set off to see what living – not vacationing – on an island in Mexico was like.

And it was just what I needed. I lived on the economy like the locals. I took the car ferry across the bay, with my tiny VW nestled between huge trucks carrying bottled water and construction materials. I shopped at the local grocery store, had to deal with handwashing my own laundry without a washer or dryer, fixed food in my tiny but adequately equipped kitchen, and lived as close to what my life would be if I decided to move.

And after five joyfully satisfying weeks, I decided to go ahead and 'pull the trigger' and I signed a year's lease to a small two-bedroom house and booked my one-way return ticket to Cancun for 60 days later. The date wasn't capricious – I either had to renew my annual lease for another year or move out of my rented home in exactly two months on the last day of the month. So I emailed my lease termination to my landlord, and flew back to San Antonio, ready to change my life forever.

Then came the hard part – actually moving OUT of the US. In comparison, moving INTO Mexico was much easier. But I won't get ahead of myself. Let's talk about you and creating your path to freedom first.

4. RUNNING TOWARDS SOMETHING GOOD

It's Not Just About Running Away From The Bad

For years, I dreamed about running away from home to live in paradise – and I've finally done it! It was the single best decision I have ever made in my life. However, it's much more than just running away FROM home, it's also about running TO a new and better life.

I've lost more than 65 pounds in the past year, with a healthy diet of fresh fruit, fish, and veggies, along with lots of shrimp ceviche, guacamole, and pico de gallo, which are island staples. I have abandoned poisonous but addictive diet sodas and enjoy cold crisp sparkling water over ice with a spritz of fresh lime instead. And I no longer drink coffee. In the past, I would need two or three cups of heavily creamed and sweetened coffee to start to function. Now I sleep deeply and wake up refreshed and ready to pull open the curtains to see the sun sparkling on the bay. And I walk a lot more - there's just more walking in Mexico and on an island - especially with a dog and an upstairs apartment!

I bought an old used car – a 2005 Chevy with manual transmission and no power steering – which gives me freedom and reliable transportation with minimum maintenance and worry. But the lifestyle here is outside, where you walk around the block to buy tortillas and fresh-squeezed orange juice. And of course, I have to walk the dog several times a day - no doggy door to the backyard. As a result, I look fifteen years younger than I did just one year ago.

When I picked a friend up at the ferry a few months ago, she couldn't recognize me. I'm a new woman, inside and out.

Today, I live on my white sandy beach. I was able to move to paradise in just two months! I live with my dog Teddy in a very comfortable two-bedroom house - Mexican style. I have a balcony with a riot of flowering plants in the front and two huge picture windows overlooking the Bay of Cancun from the spacious, high-ceilinged bedrooms. Up some very steep steps, I have a rooftop patio that is constantly caressed with ocean breezes, and where I lie in the afternoon in a comfortable beach bed, watching the sunset across shimmering turquoise water to the west.

That's when I'm not watching the sunset from Playa Norte – or North Beach – widely acclaimed as one of the nine best beaches in the world. I will be there tomorrow evening to watch the sunset and listen to opera on the beach at one of my favorite beach-front restaurants while sitting on a couch with my bare feet in the sand and my puppy in my lap.

I walk to the windswept ocean on the Caribbean side of the island every day and thank God for the chance to live in paradise. I have the time and concentration needed to build my career coaching business, on my own schedule, and I'm doing more marketing consulting – teaching marketing to Mexican entrepreneurs in different beautiful cities around Mexico – pre-pandemic of course.

Embrace a Life of Joy

Most importantly, my life is filled with joy – and music. There is always live music on the beach, streaming from upstairs balconies in nearby homes, or under the stars somewhere on the Island. I try to go by one of my favorite little music places almost every day to listen to wonderful musician friends play – Tiny Gecko, El Patio, Cocos Beach Club, the Mayan Beach Club, or Soggy Peso.

I have more friends here than I did back home, as expatriates in a foreign land bond together in an amazing way, sharing and helping and nurturing each other. Like many people who live on a small island like Isla, I support different non-profit organizations that the community benefits from – and for which we're always holding a fundraiser: the animal shelter, Red Cross, food for needy families, and more. There's the spay and neuter clinic, the diabetes clinic, art fairs, a school for handicapped children, two different college scholarship programs, and so much more. We're now supporting the construction of the Island's first university – which hopefully will start to function within a year. Everywhere I go, I run into friends, and we sit and visit with each other. What a change from being trapped inside the four walls of my home in Texas, slowly dying inside!

I have reinvented my life and finally feel free. I know my mom is being taken care of better than I could. I know she doesn't know that I'm not there. But I imagine that her spirit is sitting on my left shoulder like a tiny guardian angel, enjoying watching me live a life of joy. I know this is what she would have wanted for me and would have chosen for herself in the same situation.

The best way I can describe my life today is Joy and Peace. And it was worth all the hassles, expense, disappointments, and changes to get here.

Joy and Peace. What a gift!

I wish the same for you.

And throughout the rest of this book, I will show you how you too can run away from your current less-than-satisfying situation to find a life of joy living in your paradise – wherever your heart beats faster, and your spirit soars!

5. STARTING ON THE PATH TO FREEDOM

Discover Your Roadmap to Freedom

When I tell people where I live, they are amazed and say, "Oh my gosh, I'm so envious. I'd love to live here." Then they say "You're so brave. How did you get the nerve to leave the comfort of home and move to a foreign country?" They ask a million questions, and want to know "Weren't you scared?"

Fear is the biggest thing holding most people back from reaching their dreams.

And more than anything else, it's fear of the unknown.

So my mission is to 'pull back the curtain' to help you learn what to expect, and how to make your dream come true step-by-step.

That's why I wrote this book, to show you how it's possible to reinvent your life at any age, and to find joy in a new life that you only dreamed of before.

I will share my story, and that of others, who have successfully made the leap to their runaway lifestyle, to help show you the way. My goal is to give you hope for the future and open your eyes to the possibilities that lie ahead, and help you start on your journey of reinvention.

I invite you to visit my website www.GrownUpsGuide.com which can serve as a starting point to navigate your options to progress down the path of personal reinvention. You will find updated materials, government publications, contact information, and links to a myriad of resources that will make your move to paradise easier and less stressful than you ever imagined possible. It's your golden rolodex to all the resources to help you on your journey.

To get a good feel for life in paradise, you will definitely want to subscribe to my Facebook page at www.Facebook.com/TheGrownUpsGuideToRunningAwayFromHome. There you will find hundreds of live videos that allow you to peek into my life to get a great feel for what you might experience when you take the leap.

It's Not Forever, Just for Today

Running away from home and escaping to paradise may seem like an overwhelming challenge, and a huge forever commitment.

It takes planning and execution to make it happen successfully on your own terms. And when you know in advance what you face and how to overcome the many challenges and unknowns, it becomes easier and simpler than you ever imagined.

And while there is a lot involved in the process, you should look at it as an opportunity to transform your life for the better, not as an irreversible risk-laden choice that can't be undone

It's important to remember that your move doesn't have to be forever – it's just for today. Once you have learned how to run away from home to live in your paradise, you have gained the insights to reinvent your life when and where you want, and you are empowered to respond proactively to changes and new needs when they arise.

When people ask me how long I plan to stay here in paradise, I respond, "Until I don't want to be here anymore." It is totally liberating to know that I am in charge of my destiny, and I can live and love and celebrate life when and where and how I choose.

And now you can too.

Choosing Where to Live in Paradise

Where you choose to live is an extremely personal decision and is driven by your own wants and needs, background and history, passions and fears.

I fell in love with Isla Mujeres the first time I set foot on this tiny island, and my love affair with the island continues unabated today.

I personally think I live in the most wonderful place in the world, but lots of people in other places feel the same way. My friend, Sue, wants to move to Ajijic, which is a charming colonial village on Lake Chapala south of Guadalajara where more than 40,000 Americans and Canadians spend the winter. It's a very temperate area, with an old world look and feel, cobblestone streets, riots of colorful flowers, and beautiful guest houses set around the biggest lake in Mexico. The huge expatriate community is centered around a 50-year-old American organization called The Lake Chapala Society offering the largest English language library in Latin America, a restaurant, yoga and Spanish classes, a community center, docents who will give you an overview of the area, and lots of activities you can choose to participate in. It's lovely, and just right for Sue, but it is too expatriate-focused for me, and it doesn't have a white sandy beach, and that's important to me.

My friend Miguel is moving to tiny fishing village on the Pacific coast near Huatulco, far south of Puerto Vallarta. My digital marketing guru Lane and his wife just moved to Puerto Vallarta last month and are loving their new life in Mexico.

I know people who love Nayarit and Mazatlán and Acapulco and San Miguel de Allende and Guanajuato and Merida and Veracruz – there are so many wonderful places that speak to each person with a different song.

And it's not just Mexico. Sherri lives in Costa Rica, while James has been living in Panama for more than 10 years. Karl has a condo in a beach resort on an island in Thailand. I have friends who spend time in Puerto Rico and the Dominican Republic, so there are many places you might consider. I just think Mexico has a lot of advantages because the cost of living is so good, and you're geographically close to the United States.

Decades ago, I loved living in Portugal, Spain and Brazil, and had a wonderful life there. But at this point in my life, they feel just too far away. If something lifechanging happened like 911, or the Iceland volcano that stopped all air traffic in 2010, I couldn't get "home" to the States and family. But when you're in Mexico, you could actually get in a plane, a bus, a car or a boat and you could get home in a few hours or a couple of days by land, for whatever reason. Now with the Coronavirus travel ban, you could not fly back to the United States if you were living in Europe or Asia, but the flights have never stopped between Mexico and the US and Canada.

I have found many advantages to living in Mexico, as have more than one million other Americans who have taken up residence here - but that's my choice. Your choice can be something else. The key thing is to explore your options with an open mind. You don't have to make a rapid decision. You can take your time to think about it, but it becomes a lot less scary when you start researching and evaluating options, and slowly test the waters.

What Do You Want to Do With The Rest of Your Life?

Ask yourself, "What I want to do with the rest of my life? And where do I want to do it? Where do I feel good? Where does my heart beat faster?" To me personally, it's right here in Mexico and in Isla Mujeres. It might be someplace else for you.

And in reality, if for whatever reason I could not live here in Isla Mujeres or in Mexico, I know I would find a wonderful place to live on a white sandy beach in another country, and I would be very happy there. There are probably 20 such places if I really searched for them. But I've found my perfect home that meets all my needs, and I've put down roots, and I am extremely content to blossom where I am rooted right now.

And you can find your happy place as well. The key thing is that there is a process you can easily go through to help your figure out where you feel at home at this stage of your life, and I will walk you through the steps below.

Where Do You Want to Run Away To?

There are a number of considerations you should evaluate before homing in on a potential runaway location. Evaluate your options at the 40,000-foot level to narrow down the possibilities based on your own wants, needs, personality, and family conditions.

Here are 12 key considerations you should evaluate in advance to make sure your potential new home in paradise is a good fit:

- Affordability and Cost of Living
- Climate
- Ease of Legal Immigration
- Health Care and Medical Access
- Safety
- Lifestyle
- Culture
- Accessibility
- Urban vs. Rural Living

- Language
- Communication Infrastructure and Utilities
- Community

Let's go through them one at a time for a deeper dive.

Affordability and Cost of Living

A low cost of living is one of the key reasons people choose to run away from home to live in a foreign country. It is very difficult for anyone to survive and thrive on their pension or Social Security benefits alone – which is why you see so many mature workers greeting you at Walmart. The average US woman receives just $1,196 per month from Social Security, according to the US Census Bureau – that's less than $15,000 per year, which is well below the poverty line in the US. And with 46% of women age 65+ being single today, they can't count on a spouse's income to cover the bills.

Unfortunately, more than half of all baby boomers saw their life savings wiped out in the crash of 2007-2008, meaning they must continue to work well into their 70s to survive. That is – if they can find a job, which is extremely difficult for anyone over 55. I know; I'm a career coach. That's why I wrote my last book, **REINVENT YOUR CAREER – Beat Age Discrimination to Land Your Dream Job**. The prospect for corporate employment in the US for anyone in their late 50's, 60s or 70s is bleak – with an average of 54 weeks to find a new job for older workers – and earning 9% less than previously – if they find one at all.

For many key offshore retirement communities, the cost of living is half of what it would be in the US or Canada – and often even less, down to perhaps one third of the cost, due to low labor rates in developing countries.

A single person can live well on their meager retirement benefits in many of the overseas retirement havens. And couples with double retirement income streams can enjoy a rich life worry-free financially. You can find a nice one-bedroom apartment for as little as $400 per month in many markets, which is what you would pay for a dreary rent-subsidized HUD apartment in the States – if you can get in due to the long waiting lists.

I will pull back the curtain to detail typical cost of living numbers later in this book; for now, looking to slash your living costs in half is a great place to start.

On the other hand, you might choose a more expensive location which costs marginally less than life in the States, like Portugal or Greece, but the draw is the lifestyle and culture rather than just the lower cost of living.

Climate

Climate is a major consideration, especially if you want to live overseas full time. You want to live in a climate where you feel wonderful and can enjoy an active lifestyle. If you plan to be a snowbird, and spend only the winters overseas, you have much more climate flexibility.

I have always hated winter, cold, and snow, and have always wanted to live in the sunshine on a white sandy beach – both literally and figuratively.

Some people can't tolerate the heat of the tropics and want a more temperate climate – central Mexico towns like Lake Chapala, San Miguel de Allende, and Guanajuato are excellent options for them.

A more temperate climate can be found in southern Europe and South America in countries like Chile, Colombia, Peru and Argentina, although they also suffer cold winters during June, July,

August and September – just the opposite of our seasons. Few people realize that the southern European capitals of Madrid, Rome and Athens are at almost the same latitude as New York City, and may not be aware of the fact that their winters can be very cold, close to freezing. When I lived in Madrid, Spain, I learned to snow ski in the Sierra Nevada mountains just north of the city. You don't often think of it, but the Alps are in northern Italy. Make sure you visit your dream destination in different seasons to get a complete picture of the seasonal extremes.

Closely related to climate are seasonal allergies. The clear ocean breezes of the tropics tend to prevent airborne allergies, but if you choose to live in more temperate areas, you might find you are allergic to trees like ash or cedar, or grasses and plants. If you have never experienced severe hay fever, you don't realize the importance of climate in terms of avoiding allergies.

Ease of Legal Immigration

Another key consideration is the ease of establishing residency in your new home country, and it varies widely around the globe. While some countries like New Zealand and Australia have extremely high thresholds for immigration, many other countries actively woo foreigners to move there to stimulate the local economy.

That's the case in Mexico, where all you need is a US or Canadian passport to be given a six-month tourist visa. After 180 days, you must leave the country, but can return in just a few days and gain another six-month visa. I've recently spoken to friends who were able to circumvent the need to leave the country, as the Mexican immigration office is provisionally allowing expats to renew their visa in Mexico rather than being forced to leave – it's a great accommodation brought on due to the pandemic.

To become a resident, you need to apply at your local consulate in your home country and demonstrate that you have the financial assets to support yourself while in the country. With around $32,000 of liquid assets in a bank, savings or investment account, or a monthly pension of about $1,950 per month, you can earn a Temporary residency visa, which you renew annually without additional proof of income. To become a Permanent resident, you simply have to demonstrate liquid assets of approximately $130,000, or a monthly income of abou t$3,200. We will talk more about the requirements to move to Mexico in a later chapter.

Other countries like Belize, Costa Rica, Panama, Guatemala and several Caribbean islands actively seek foreign immigrants, and some even offer incentives. Likewise, Portugal and Greece make it very easy to become a legal resident, and there is a small town in Italy that will actually pay you to move there and buy a house or start a business.

Health Care and Medical Access

We tend to consider our US or Canadian medical system to be the best in the world, but you will be surprised with how affordable and accessible good health care can be in overseas locations.

Driven by low labor costs and government subsidies, you will find local health care services to be very inexpensive – a small fraction of the cost of comparable services in the US.

Here in Mexico, you don't need a prescription to purchase most medicines, and the pharmacists actually consult with patients to recommend needed medications, which are priced at a tiny percentage of US costs. Many pharmacy chains offer a "doc in a box" – a private doctor who sees walk-in patients in an office adjacent to the pharmacy, and a consultation costs around $2! The doctor will prescribe needed medicines and will give shots as needed.

A year ago, I got a terrible cold while traveling to Mexico City, and I was absolutely miserable. I found a local pharmacy with a doctor's clinic attached. I walked right in, had my vitals taken and a physical exam, and told the doctor about my symptoms. In just 20 minutes, I walked out with a steroid shot to start a rapid recovery, and a C-pack of antibiotics, a bottle of strong cough medicine, and an analgesic for the pain and discomfort – and it all cost less than $25.

Access to your own doctor is easy and incredibly inexpensive as well. I go to a British-trained doctor, Dr. Greta, who has 30 years of experience practicing here in Mexico and also in Abu Dhabi, and is a family care doctor, gynecologist, and a tropical disease specialist. A visit to her office costs $25, and an appointment is not needed. She takes calls and text messages on her mobile phone and makes home visits when necessary or convenient.

Dr. Salas is a Mexican doctor who speaks perfect English. He worked for 15 years for the Navy as the head at the local naval hospital before setting up his own private practice and offers similar rates. He also provides holistic treatments like chelation, homeopathic medicines, a med spa, and also works half a day at a clinic for government employees. He recently arranged to have me medically evacuated from the island in the middle of the night by water ambulance when my appendix ruptured late on a Sunday evening. Seven hours later, I had emergency surgery by a well-trained surgeon who speaks perfect English in a modern 24-hour surgical hospital – and it was all paid for by my medical insurance.

My chiropractor, Dr. Ben, is a Belgian chiropractor who set up and ran the Chiropractic School of Veracruz for more than 20 years, before moving to Isla a year ago. His appointments cost $25 – and his office is currently a covered deck nestled in the branches of a Banyan tree at the oldest marina on the island! It looks like a scene out of the Disney classic The Swiss Family Robinson. I absolutely love it!

Dental care is likewise excellent and inexpensive. Doctora Victoria has a small dental office, and charges about one third of what it would cost for comparable service in the States. Cleaning is less than $30, and a porcelain crown costs around $250.

These are the services I can find in my tiny Island of 5,000 people. In Cancun, there are a number of state-of-the-art and internationally certified hospitals, and dozens of esteemed doctors who have studied medicine at leading medical schools both in Mexico and in the US.

Mexico and other countries offer bustling medical tourism business. My friend Keesha just had major plastic surgery – a breast reduction, tummy tuck, liposuction all over, arm reduction – and it cost $4,600. Another friend, Paula, had a complete face lift for $3,300 – less than 20 percent of what it would have cost in the States. And my friends Trinna and Murry each had a full set of dental veneers for $1,000 each. I accompanied Jackie on her visits to three different dental clinics for exams, X rays, and quotes for dental implants of six teeth – and the quotes ranged from $3,000 to $4,200 – what you might pay for just one implant in the US.

Other popular expatriate locations offer similar excellent medical care at amazingly low rates.

And I connected with a woman who came to Cancun to a holistic cancer treatment center for her Stage 4 cancer – and was cured in just two months and now lives cancer-free in Minnesota.

I recently noticed that my vision was getting blurry, so I booked an appointment with an ophthalmologist in Cancun. The eye exam was $15, and a full consultation with the doctor was another $20. Irregularities in the exam indicated I needed a more detailed computer scan of the retina, and I went right to a private vision center

THE GROWNUPS GUIDE TO RUNNING AWAY FROM HOME

where I had detailed retina scans of both eyes for just under $100 – cash. I scheduled YAG laser surgery to remove film on my implanted lenses and paid $300 again in cash for treatment of both eyes, scheduled at my convenience within a week. According to MDSave, the comparable cost in the US averages $2,376 for private pay without Medicare.

Because of the incredibly low costs, in many cases you have better and faster access to quality medical care overseas than in our bureaucratic medical system with long wait times, in-patient provider networks, huge medical insurance costs and outrageous deductibles, and the need for referrals from a primary care physician.

While traditional Medicare does not cover any procedures outside the US, a number of Medicare Advantage plans and private insurance will reimburse emergency care, so self-insuring your day-to-day medical costs on the local economy is a great option.

I have Medicare Complete Advantage Plan with United Health Care, which paid for my full appendix surgery and treatment as an emergency. If I had a major medical emergency and I wanted it treated in the States for full payment coverage, I could be in Houston, Miami or San Antonio on a direct flight within a few hours.

There are overseas medical insurance plans, and medevac policies which can provide needed peace of mind if you are concerned about the cost and treatment options of major medical issues. Visit Resources section of my web page www.GrownUpsGuide.com for an updated list of providers, hospitals and insurance options that can help you meet your medical needs very economically.

Safety

Physical safety is a very important consideration in moving overseas, and you should check out safety at the local as well as national level.

But don't just look at the stats – ask the locals you meet or connect with online for their perception of the local situation.

In the United States, there are areas of Los Angeles, Chicago and New York that you would not go into alone or at night, and it is the same overseas.

If you avoid high risk activities – like buying drugs or illegal guns, going to strip clubs or engaging in prostitution – most tourists and expat travelers find the local communities to be very safe.

At the same time, areas catering to tourism place a premium on visitor safety, and make sure tourist areas are heavily policed. Here is Isla, there are actually Tourist Police representatives who are dispatched on motorcycles to help track down lost phones and stolen passports and investigate complaints by victims to gain quick relief.

I personally feel much safer here in Mexico and in Isla Mujeres than I do in the States. I have little fear of burglary or assault, and I drive all over the island day and night with no concern for my safety. Having my puppy Teddy by my side of course provides comfort and reassurance, and I choose to live in a neighborhood where people know what's going on, know each other, and would instantly spot any dangerous or suspicious activity.

I am also reassured rather than alarmed by the large number of police personnel from three different organizations – the local police force, the naval MPs, and the federal police force – all carrying pistols or machine guns. They patrol the streets on foot, as well as from the back of trucks, and come out in force during special events and holidays to ensure the economic activity of the island – tourism – is not harmed by crime.

I was also surprised and reassured to learn that most businesses have security cameras functioning, and can track thefts or fraud, and will provide screen capture of crime suspects on social media to help track down perpetrators.

That doesn't mean that crime doesn't exist, just like crime exists where you live today. Fortunately, most crimes I've heard about (but have not experienced myself) have been property theft. A non-Mexican stole the wallet from my friend Melissa's purse while she was giving her a lift in the back seat of her car. The bar owner where they met provided images of the suspect, and Melissa was able to post the image of the blonde woman on Facebook – and she evidently disappeared quickly from the island when everyone knew who she was.

I was greatly overcharged at a local supermarket when buying supplies for a fishing trip with a group of people. Accompanied by a local friend, I took the receipt to the store manager, and he reviewed the security camera footage, verified that I was overcharged, and issued me a full refund on the spot.

At this point, I have never heard of any foreigner who was attacked, raped or physically harmed in all the time I have lived here.

Likewise, everyone is cautioned to use common sense – don't wear expensive jewelry, flash lots of money around, stagger drunk down the street at night, or go into questionable areas of big cities like Cancun at night. It's the same advice you would get in any city or town in America.

Lifestyle Choices

Where you are at this point in your life will determine the kind of lifestyle you are seeking. Are you interested in going out and dancing in nightclubs all night? Or are you happy to have a glass of wine on the rooftop and watch the sun set while visiting with friends? After 20, 30, 40 or more years of working hard, many people want to slow down a little bit and smell the roses. Or you may be seeking the stimulation of a new location, a new culture, and want to strike out in adventure after decades of caring for family, home and job.

The type and intensity of activities you aspire to engage in will impact your choice of where to move. Some people may want a retirement life centered around a golf course, while others want their lives focused on grandchildren, or starting a passion project, or learning new skills.

Do you crave beach time, ocean activities, swimming, snorkeling, scuba, fishing, or sailing? Then a white sandy beach might be perfect for you.

If golf is your passion, you will want to choose a different tropical or temperate location. If you want to snow ski for months on end, you will likewise choose in a colder mountainous region.

The kind of activities you engage in are an important lifestyle choice, and one of the common characteristics of living overseas in paradise is a more active, outgoing, outdoor lifestyle. You will want to research the type of activities that are available, and determine if they are free, reasonably priced, or expensive.

I know that 30 years ago, Isla Mujeres would have been too small for me. I craved living in a vibrant capital of Europe and progressing in my business career with major companies in their headquarters locations. But today, this pace is just right for me. Your needs and preferences may well shift as you age and change.

My friends Dawn and Tom relocated three times before getting it right. They wanted to escape from high cost, high tax, and high stress southern California, and moved first to Panama City in the Florida panhandle with their 48-foot sailboat – a small luxury yacht really. They found it to be too touristy at the beach, and too blue collar in the suburbs, with all their neighbors working at the nearby naval base.

They also didn't enjoy the cold winters compared to other parts of Florida. After two years, they moved again to Port Charlotte in southwestern Florida. They felt it to be too slow-paced, and were bored with the snowbird retiree lifestyle, where the idea of "Let's go out for dinner Friday night" meant joining another couple for an early bird special at 5 p.m. at a Perkins or Cracker Barrel restaurant. They finally sailed their yacht The Santorini to Isla Mujeres, where they found an enjoyable active outdoor community with a rich network of engaged expats from all over the world. They decided to set down roots and bought a property which they remodeled into a beautiful 4-suite guesthouse perched on the seawall, or 'malecon' next to the Caribbean Sea in the popular downtown area, commanding premium rental prices. They have recently added a third-floor owner's suite and live there full time. They are now considering selling their boat, as their needs have changed with the years.

This highlights the need to find a place to live that "feels" right to you today, where your find yourself right now, and one that provides the right balance of stimulation, adventure, and community to create the lifestyle of your dreams.

Culture

Each city and region has a unique culture, and you have the option of choosing to live in the culture that you find stimulating, welcoming, and attractive.

Different parts of the United States and Canada each have their unique culture, just like Mexico and other countries do. The laid-back vibe of Southern California is very different from the party mentality of New Orleans, or the urban sophistication of New York or Chicago. Life in Miami is very different from life in Minneapolis or Vermont. Someone hailing from Montana or Texas might not appreciate the southern lifestyle of Atlanta or rural Georgia or North Carolina.

One of the great opportunities of moving overseas is to explore the unique culture of the area, and the unique characteristics of the people who live there, which will probably be an exciting new experience to you.

Of course, you want to live around people that you enjoy, and you want to savor their history, religion, art, music, and local customs and traditions of your adopted land. I personally enjoy Mexico because I really love the Mexican people. But I have discovered that the Yucatan has a unique Mayan culture and influence which is very notable and different from other parts of Mexico. The food, language, location names, even the architecture and home construction, art, and local traditions are uniquely Mayan, which is a fascinating experience which I am enjoying very much.

Make sure your new home offers you a culture you will enjoy living in and exploring, as part of the richness of your overseas lifestyle.

Accessibility

Another key consideration is how easily accessible your new location is for travel and needed services. You may plan to go back to visit family and friends in the States or Canada a couple of times a year, and you probably want loved ones to visit you on their holidays. Travel times, distance, costs, and accessibility to a great airport are key considerations. I know the Philippines and Thailand are wonderful retirement spots, but travel there is overwhelming – it may take 24 hours or more, with multiple transfers or layovers, and often costs thousands of dollars to get there.

When I lived in Europe, it took a full day and sometimes two to get to my home in southern Florida. It was a six-hour flight from Lisbon to New York, and often the flight would arrive late, and I would be stranded overnight in JFK airport sleeping on the floor of the terminal. Then I would fly to Atlanta, and then take a connecting flight to Ft. Myers in south Florida, often arriving the next afternoon. And it took days to recover from jet lag due to the time zone change.

Living in Mexico, I can be at the Cancun airport in 2 hours, and then it's a two-hour direct flight to many major cities, or a few more hours if I have to catch a connecting flight. And the cost is low – I routinely book round trip flights from Cancun to San Antonio for $400, which is less than what I used to pay to visit my son in Portland, Oregon from San Antonio. If cost is the driving factor, you can find many promotional or last-minute flights with longer flight times but cheap prices if you are looking for costs savings.

Time zones are important for communication, and one of the great things about Mexico is it has the same 4 time zones as the US, so it's easy to be connected to work and family and services. When I lived in Europe, there was just a short time window for placing phone calls or connecting online with the office. And my friends who live in New Zealand and Australia have to get up in the middle of their night for business conference calls and to talk to doctors, financial advisors, or family and friends.

Urban vs Rural Living – Or the Best of Both Worlds

Do you want to live in a big bustling city, with great shopping, restaurants, fine grocery stores, art galleries, theaters, private hospitals, and a major airport for travel convenience? Or would you prefer a smaller town filled with charm and a slower pace of life, but without some of the conveniences of a larger city? You may choose somewhere in between – a smaller town within an hour's drive of a big city, so you can get the services and products you want within a reasonable drive time.

That's one of the great things I love about Isla Mujeres. The island is quaint and charming, with a small hometown feel, despite the huge influx of tourists from Christmas through Easter. But Cancun is just a 17-minute ferry ride away, with a world class international airport that connects to virtually every major city on the globe. Flying to Houston or Miami is a 2-hour non-stop flight, and fares are reasonable. And there are direct non-stop flights to every major city of the US, Canada, and the rest of the world from the Cancun airport. Cancun offers all the conveniences of home, including all your favorite big box stores – Costco and Sam's, Wal-Mart, Office Depot, Home Depot, PetSmart, and all the high-end fashion retailers – you name it. That's in addition to all the Mexican stores.

Other favorite tourist areas offer a similar blend of small town feel with big city access. The Lake Chapala area, with an expatriate community of more than 40,000, is just an hour's drive from a major airport for Mexico's second largest city, Guadalajara. Cuernavaca is a charming resort area an hour from Mexico City, with a year-round temperate garden-like climate. Other popular tourist areas, like Acapulco, Puerto Vallarta, and Cabo San Lucas, are a bit farther away from the major urban areas and may require a long drive or a connecting flight to get there, increasing costs and travel times, and limiting visits to consulates and major retail and medical centers.

And there are many other cities and resort areas in Mexico where you can easily drive your own car from the States, such as Cabo San Lucas and La Paz in Baja California, or down the Pacific Coast of Mexico to Mazatlán, Puerto Vallarta, Manzanillo, and Acapulco. Puerto Peñasco is just south of Tucson, easily accessible by car. And some intrepid souls drive down the Gulf coast to Campeche, Tampico or Veracruz, before heading southeast on the Yucatan peninsula to Cancun.

And if you want the hustle, bustle and vibrant business, arts, and entertainment of a major city, you have many to choose from. Monterrey in northern Mexico, just a 5-hour drive from San Antonio in Texas, has a population of more than one million. Guadalajara, further south and west near Puerto Vallarta, in the northwest colonial region of the country, has more than seven million residents. And of course, the capital of Mexico City is a huge metropolis, with more than 21 million residents, similar to the size of New York City. And all around these major markets, you will find dozens of smaller towns and villages loaded with charm or providing upscale living conditions and offering the best of both worlds.

Language

While there are a number of countries where English is commonly spoken, like Belize, Australia, The Philippines, and India, the vast majority of potential relocation areas require you to communicate in the native language to really fit in. In tourist areas, you will find it much easier to communicate in English than in rural areas which don't get a lot of tourist traffic. You may want to choose a country with a language which is easy to learn – like Spanish, Portuguese, French or Italian. I've traveled to many countries, and I can't imagine the challenges of trying to learn Greek, Russian, Czech, Thai, Chinese, Japanese or Arabic. Imagine having to learn a whole different alphabet - or writing right to left!

And while speaking the language may not be necessary, it really enriches your experience in the country of your choice. You can connect with locals, get things done easily, meet and really connect with friends who don't speak English, and truly enjoy the culture – including the arts, theater, music, history, archeology and so much more. Therefore, you may want to choose a location where the language is easy to learn.

Many of us studied Spanish in high school, and it may be easier to dust off long-forgotten Spanish grammar than to learn a whole new language. More than 350 million people speak Spanish in the world, more than speak English, so it's a much more versatile language than French, German or Italian, which offer many fewer opportunities to use it.

Communication Infrastructure and Utilities

In today's world, it is important that you find good overall communication infrastructure, especially if you plan to work while living in paradise.

Many developing countries have leapfrogged over traditional buried copper cable phone lines to offer vibrant cellular phone service and digital internet services at very low rates.

Here in Mexico, cellular phone service is very inexpensive, and you can buy a phone and airtime at local supermarkets and convenience stores. Many Mexicans do not have credit facilities, so they pay for airtime with prepaid cards or load time onto their phones as needed.

Many markets offer high speed internet by satellite or fiber cable, and you can access a wide array of services with smart TVs and mobile technology. Everyone has Netflix, and you can access your US account through your computer or a VPN to watch English language television programs. You can also use an Amazon Fire Stick or your Hulu or Netflix TV account to access US programs. Amazon offers a full suite of movies, TV shows and music as part of its Amazon Prime service for just $100 per year – a real steal And I recently subscribed to Express VPN, which gives much more versatile internet access, and comes with dozens of free channels, including most broadcast TV channels.

It's good to know that the electric system in Mexico is the same as in the US, and you don't need plug adaptors or voltage transformers to run your US-sourced electronics. When I lived in Portugal, the electric system featured round plugs on all outlets that were 220 current, and 50 cycles instead of 60 cycles like in the US, and it was a hassle to have to use special plug adaptors and bulky transformers on all appliances. Today, with the prevalence of contemporary electronics, computers, mobile phones and tablets, you may want to live in a place where you are not at risk of electric current differences. Make sure you check out the electric requirements before making a final decision.

Community

What kind of a community will you choose to live in? Do you want to live in an expat community, like Tulum or Ajijic, or in Belize, where the majority of the residents are foreigners? Will you choose an upscale gated community for safety and prestige, and perhaps a year-round golf course? Or do you want to live among the locals, buy your groceries at neighborhood stores and from street vendors, and become friends with your neighbors? You get to choose.

One of the things that I love about living overseas is the bond of friendship that is created when you are far from home and need to build a new network of friends. These bonds can be created with other expats from many countries in addition to your own, as well as the local residents themselves, but they can be formidable.

When you move into a new community in the States, you may find that most of the people you meet already have a fully packed social network of family members, longtime friends, coworkers and neighbors they have known for years, and are less open to forming strong bonds with a new arrival. Their 'friend receptors' are all full. They are busy living their active lives, and they don't have a lot of need or bandwidth to add a new person to their close network of friends.

When you arrive in a new country, however, you will meet up with other adventuresome souls like yourself, and you will meet people who are open and available to build new bonds of friendship. They probably have several empty 'friend receptors' so you can bond instantly due to so many common factors – often caused by your choice to move to paradise. You will also find that longer time residents are helpful in reaching out and providing friendship, since they have previously made the same life choices you did, and they remember how challenging and confusing it may have been at first. Helping you makes them feel good, so it's a win-win.

Having lived abroad for a number of years in four different countries, I have found that you want a community of both fellow expats and locals.

Your expat community will provide you with the comfort of home – the ability to express yourself freely in your native language, shared customs, comfort food, familiar expectations, and the ability to open up and vent about the many tiny yet bothersome irritants in your day-to-day life. You may create lifelong friends from your expat neighbors and new acquaintances.

Your local friends will provide you with help, connections, answers to questions, and can protect you from harm and exploitation. I have become good friends with my next-door neighbors Zoila and Rogelio. They invite me to their house for dinners and special meals with their extended family, and I invite them to my home for parties and social activities. When I decided to leave for a few days to avoid an imminent hurricane, I left the keys to my home with them, and they took in the plants, fed and cleaned up after the kitties, and made sure my house was ready to bear the onslaught of what we expected to be massive winds. When the storm had passed, they put everything back in place, cleaned the house, and even washed the salty storm water off the windows and the sliding glass door.

When Rogelio drove me to the ferry for my trip off the island, he noted that my car needed serious repairs. With my approval, he took my car to his mechanic, had major repairs done, and made sure the bill was incredibly small – I know it was less than half of what I would have been charged as a foreigner, and a tiny fraction of what I would have paid in the States.

When I had surgery in Cancun recently, Zoila came with me and checked me out of the hospital and stayed in the hotel with me for two days to make sure I was all right overnight, and tended to my post-surgery needs. Then Rogelio brought my car over so I could return to our island seated in the car on the car ferry, rather than standing in line to board the regular passenger ferry with my luggage in the open air. That's great friendship.

And it's a two-way street. When their 20-year-old son was planning to go to the US to visit his older brother, I made sure he had $50 in small bills to use for tips, to buy snacks and meals, and to meet his personal needs while traveling for a day. I helped Rogelio build his LinkedIn page and write his resume so he could apply for a new job, and I created beautiful business cards and a business Facebook page to help Zoila grow her manicure business. When their electric transformer was blown, we ran a 40-foot electric cord from a wall socket in my bathroom out   the window down to the ground floor, where they could pull it into their house and power their refrigerator and lights for a week until the electric service was restored.

It's great to know that I have someone who will look out for me, make sure I am not gouged by tourist prices, and help me get things done – like setting up an appointment to get my car title transferred in the middle of the pandemic when the government office was closed. Everyone needs at least one resourceful local friend and supporter who can be counted on to cover your back and help you find you way in a foreign land. Besides that, they are wonderful people, and you will enjoy their friendship and exchanging insight into cultural differences to make your life in paradise even more enjoyable and worry-free.

Decide What You Want from Paradise

Now's the time to figure out exactly what you want your dream life to be like and claim it for yourself. If you don't have a crystal-clear vision of what you want to achieve, it simply won't come true. Your mind, and the magical universe, works in a miraculous way to act on your strongly expressed positive desires, and make them become your reality.

Here are four different ways to help you make your dreams come true. And they are all free, and easy to do:

Create Your Criteria for the Future Using Your Paradise Dreamsheet

By now you should have a pretty comprehensive list of criteria to help you define what your Paradise will look like. Download the Dreamsheet from my website www.GrownUpsGuide.com – look for the Resource section – and it will guide you through the 12 different criteria you should consider to help you create your vision of your dream life in the future. For each of the 12 items on the list we just discussed, write down exactly what you want in your new life in paradise, for each topic.

If you are planning to travel with a partner or family members, ask each person to write down their wish list in private, then perhaps have a fun evening sharing your lists to see what you have chosen in common – and to discuss areas where your vision diverges. Do some soul searching. Close your eyes and visualize what you want your new life to be like.

Then take the time to go through the list and rank or prioritize the items. You may find everything you want. Or like most things in life, you may have to compromise a bit. Separating the "Must Haves" from the "Nice to Haves" will be helpful.

Create Your Dream Board

Then create a dream board to visually represent your future life. There is an amazing power in visually representing your intentions. It actually compels the universe to make your dream come true. In the past I clipped pictures and words from a magazine to paste onto a big posterboard to depict my dream life. Today I simply open a new PowerPoint slide and find and paste images from the web that show my vision for the future. It's that easy. Save the slide in a jpg image and as a pdf and print out copies to post where you will see them often in your home and car. Save it as a screen saver on your computer and phone so it will always be present in your life. If your dream changes, or when you achieve a goal and want to add a new one in its place, it's as easy as editing your PowerPoint file and saving a new version. Look at your dream board daily and congratulate yourself for having such a wonderful life. Visualize it as already being your life to allow it to come true. See examples and simple directions at my website www.GrownUpsGuide.com – look for the Resources section.

Describe A Day in Your Life in Paradise

Next create a written snapshot of a future day in paradise – just like I shared with you in the prologue of this book. Use all five senses to powerfully describe your typical day in paradise and express the emotions that you feel. Write it in present tense, visualizing it in the future, whether one year or five years from now, and use lots of adjectives or descriptive words to paint a word picture that will make your dream life sound and feel real and tangible.

Lastly, Change the Way Your Talk About Your Future – and Everything Else

Many people sabotage their dreams and plans by the language they use, totally unaware that they are sending the absolutely wrong message to the universe. Your subconscious mind can't tell the difference between a positive and negative statement and will give you what it hears you ask for. If you say, "I will never have enough money to retire," you won't. If you say, "I will die working at this job", you probably will. If you say, "All I meet are lousy cheating men who are broke and drink too much", you have just told the universe that is what you want. If you say "I will never lose weight and I will be fat the rest of my life," your subconscious mind will hear that as your desire – and will give it to you.

Instead, state exactly what you DO want, clearly and concisely, and never say what you DON'T want. Whenever you hear yourself state a negative outcome, restate it in a positive manner, several times, to erase your unconsciously sabotaging message.

Soon you will hear how other people are creating their future, good or bad, with their words. I have a dear friend who has struggled with just about everything in life – jobs, money, kids, relationships, weight – you name it. Whenever I talk to her, she wails about how awful her life is. All I hear is "I hate my job. I'll never make enough money to retire. My house is falling down around my shoulders, and I don't have enough money to fix it. My car is on its last legs, and I can't afford to buy a new one. I don't think my sons will ever leave home. I'm going to have to settle for a lousy job at a dollar store as I can't pay my bills. Whenever I apply for a job, I get turned down because

I'm too old and weigh too much. Every time I try to lose weight, I end up gaining more weight and I hate myself because I'm fat." She doesn't realize that she is clearly telling the universe what her future should be, and sure enough, it's exactly what she gets, over and over again. When I ask her to say something positive, she says there is nothing positive about her life. At this point I find it hard to even pick up the phone to call her, as I know I will be bombarded with negativity and self-defeating declarations, and she won't listen to my attempts to help her. Don't let this be your future. Change how you talk about your life, talking only in a positive manner, in present tense, declaring your intentions, so they can come true.

Follow these four exercises, and clearly paint a vision of your future. Then with your vision of life in paradise firmly anchored in your mind and heart, get ready to start doing your research to find the perfect place for you.

6. DO YOUR RESEARCH TO FIND YOUR PARADISE

The next step in your journey to freedom is to start doing your research to identify the perfect location of your paradise.

Make an extensive list of the locations you would consider for your future life. It may be a short or longer list – it's up to you.

You may be lucky, and already have a crystal-clear vision of where you want to be – like I did. That makes it so much simpler. But if not, start by doing research to home in on several ideal locations.

Get Help From The CIA

A great resource to help you drill down on your options is a little-known publication – The CIA World Factbook. You can access it in the Resource section of my website www.GrownUpsGuide.com . I've downloaded the current report for Mexico there, so it's at your fingertip, as well as a link to the whole site.

It provides constantly updated extremely detailed reports on every country in the world, covering many of the items on your checklist, making it easy to read and comprehend. Download the report for each country on your target list to a folder on your computer to be gathering the data to help you on your way.

Publications

There are lots of books, magazines, and online pages and newsletters that can provide priceless information to help you create your future life overseas. Here are some of my favorites:

International Living Magazine

The best publication I have come across to help you explore life overseas is the International Living Magazine. Go to my website at www.GrownUpsGuide.com for the link which often offers a special discount. An annual subscription is just $17, and includes six bi-monthly printed issues, and an emailed online version as well. They have many different programs, conferences, white papers, emailed postcards, investment programs…the works. I found it very helpful while starting to plan my move overseas. The publication provides a wealth of information to get you focusing on locations you might not have thought of before. And the magazine profiles many people in their overseas life so you can put yourself in their shoes to visualize the kind of lifestyle you want.

Books and Travel Guides

There are literally hundreds of books relating to overseas living, international living, retiring abroad, living in Mexico, etc. and you will find many of them to be relevant or of interest.

My companion book to this one, to be published in the fall, is called **The Runaway Roadmap: Your Step-by-Step Guide to Escape to Paradise and Live Richly on Any Budget.** In that book, and the workbook by the same name, I detail the nitty gritty details of each step of your plan to move to paradise. I've given you an overview of the considerations and key steps in this book, but there's just not enough time or space to detail it all here without getting so bogged down and overwhelmed with the minutiae you will need when you actually start your move. This second book will help you make your move faster and easier than you ever imagined possible. It's available on Amazon, as well as on my website www.GrownUpsGuide.

A popular book offering great insight is **Why We Left - An Anthology of American Women Expats**, by Janet Blazer. It details the lives of 27

American women who have moved to different parts of Mexico, and their reasons for doing so.

Of course, you should read – or re-read – **The 4-Hour Work Week** by Tim Ferriss, which brought awareness to the idea that you could live overseas and build a portable easy-to-manage online income stream as far back as 2007.

There is an almost infinite number of books that can help you in your journey of transformation, each providing different information, perspectives, and stories. Enjoy the armchair journey to help you prepare for the physical journey.

These books, and many more, are available on my website at www.TheGrownUpsGuide.com. You have lots of stimulating reading ahead of you.

Podcasts

Enjoy the podcast of my friend, Dawn Fleming, called Overseas Life Redesign. Dawn has been interviewing a wide range of people who have chosen to live overseas, many here in Isla Mujeres, as well as in other locations. I was her fifth interview back in 2019, and you can learn about my transformation over the years, as well as those of other friends you may meet in your move to paradise.

Facebook Groups

Today, one of the single best ways to research prospective locations is to subscribe to the myriad Facebook groups by and about people who live in your desired destination. There may be dozens of pages and groups. Search for the location name in Facebook and find as many groups as possible and join them. Follow the groups, learn about seasons and activities, and get to know people and locations remotely.

More than a year before I seriously started to plan my move, I created both a physical and a computer file, and tucked in there everything I could find about Mexico and Isla Mujeres specifically. I jotted down names of restaurants, hotels, venues, tours, clubs and nonprofit organizations, and activities to check out when I got here. I learned who was active, who responded to requests for information, and who offered to help. You can quickly get the lay of the land that way.

Local Social or Meet Up Groups

Overseas living is a very social lifestyle, and the result is many different local groups of expats or residents in different areas or with different interests. Many of them will have Facebook pages or groups where you can learn about local opportunities to meet and connect in person.

Some will be centered around work or business, others about charities and non-profits, or varied interests and passions. I studied international business in graduate school, and the university has a huge alumni organization with local meetings around the world where alums meet monthly face to face, and instantly bond due to shared backgrounds and interests. Check out your school's alumni association to see who might be living in your dream location. It's easy to find local alumni groups on Facebook, which is a great place to start, and then move on to researching opportunities to meet people in person.

There may be Meet Up Groups in your desired destination, which may be another option for meeting people with similar interests or located in your target destination, so check to see what they offer.

Tap Into Personal Networks

I am a working professional, so business and job information were important to me. I tapped into my graduate school alumni network, and LinkedIn, to try to identify people who currently or previously lived where I was headed. You can always post questions and requests for help on Facebook – you will be amazed by the number of people you know who may have a connection to your desired location. Since I moved here to this tiny island, I have met more than a dozen people who either moved here from San Antonio, or currently live there and vacation here frequently. They are great resources for bringing down mail, medicines and special hard-to-find treasures on their frequent visits back home.

Government Resources

And of course, you can find a wealth of information through the governments of both your own country and your destination country.

On my website www.GrownUpsGuide, you will find lots of updated information and links to valuable resources, including:

- The CIA World Factbook
- US Secretary of State
- Mexican Secretary of State website
- Mexican Consulate Website – website for immigration information

Make sure you visit the Resource section of www.GrownUpsGuide.com for up-to-date information about all aspects of your future relocation, including immigration issues.

You can also download my own Ultimate Guide to Moving to Mexico, at http://www.YourImmigrationGuideToMexico.com/.

Now that you've done your research and narrowed down the potential list of future locations, you can start to vacation with a purpose – to help you find your paradise.

7. VACATION WITH A PURPOSE

The next phase of your journey may be to vacation with a purpose – take vacation time and visit your potential dream locations to try them on for size.

I visited Isla five times over a four-year period before I finally decided to move here. And in between trips to Isla, I twice vacationed in Puerto Vallarta as a guest of friends in their lovely timeshare.

For some reason, Puerto Vallarta never resonated with me. The beaches were grittier than the powder white sand of North Beach. The water was not as warm. There was only one view – looking west – compared to the 365-degree views of my island. But I kept traveling and comparing each new location to my island benchmark.

And every time I traveled, I met people and picked their brains. I went out of my way to meet other expats and ask them dozens of probing questions – what they liked and didn't like, how much their rent was, what kind of visa they were on, what they did for work or entertainment, how they handled banking and phone service, and so much more.

Take as many vacation trips as possible to many different locations until you find the one location you always want to go back to over and over again. These don't have to be long trips – you will have a good feel for the location in a week to 10 days if you get out and meet people and do you 'flipflops in the sand' research. If possible, vacation in the type of housing you might live in when you move there. Don't go to an all-inclusive resort. Instead, rent an Airbnb apartment and get a feel for how to live on the economy, to cook your own meals, do your own shopping, wash your own laundry. Strategically visit the places on your short list and go through the Runaway Checklist to critically analyze the 12 key criteria from Chapter 5.

How Does It Feel?

When you vacation with a purpose, tap into your feelings – how do you feel? Are you excited, stimulated, filled with joy?

Are you bothered by the inconveniences? Or are you thrilled with the adventure?

Do your allergies get worse – or disappear in the ocean breeze?

Do you enjoy getting out and walking around, looking at everything from street level – especially if you live like a couch potato at home?

When you find that one special place you are drawn to over and over again, and when it passes your checklist, it will probably be time to do a Beta Test.

Do Your Beta Test

For years, I've been saying that as soon as I could, I would run away from home to live in Isla Mujeres. For a long time, it was a dream, a fantasy.

But I wanted to make it real!

So 2019 was the year! I knew that if I didn't do it then, it would be another year, and then another and I might never get to live my dream.

I did my Beta Test – and never looked back.

When we speak of a Beta Test, we often think of a software pre-launch test - but basically, it means a dry run or a test drive. It's a trial to see if a new program or product will work. That said, there are some things you need to do while running your Beta Test process to ensure it is successful and you get the results you desire. Remember the checklist in Chapter 5 to help you home in on your ideal market? You will have the opportunity to put those insights into action, and learn for yourself what is important to you, and whether your Beta Test location is the right destination for you.

Your Beta Test is a low-risk trial, where the worst thing that could happen is that you may have wasted a month and a couple of thousand dollars...on a white sandy beach...in paradise.

On my Beta Test, I learned everything that I needed to know. I met lots of people and asked lots of questions. I visited doctors and chiropractors and dentists and vets to make sure that I had the necessary health resources lined up. I looked at many different housing options in different parts of the island, to see what it would cost, and if I would be happy living in that lifestyle. And I continued to work professionally as a career coach and author and marketing consultant, because I was able to rent an apartment with good Wi-Fi and Netflix - what else did I need?

What Do You Want to Get Out of Your Beta Test?

The goal of your Beta Test is to gain clarity – is this doable or not? Is this something that will work at this phase in your life?

A well-executed Beta Test should take away the unknowns and the fear that comes with them and give you the insights into whether this is your ideal life solution – for you and your family.

And it allows you to make decisions and take action. That action might be the decision to sell everything and head out now to live in paradise. It might also be the decision that, as nice as it is, this is not the right place for you.

There are no right or wrong answers. If you decide that this isn't the perfect solution, it frees you up to move on and find your optimal solution. So in this way, your Beta Test is a win-win. You win if you find paradise. And you win if you are freed up to try something else.

Remember, the worst thing that can happen on your Beta Test in a less-than-perfect vacation. So don't overthink it. Just do it and move on to the next phase.

When Should You Do Your Beta Test?

The simple answers it – as soon as possible. But that means after you have done your preliminary research and homed in on one or more desired locations.

You should do your Beta Text at a different time of the year than when you so happily vacationed in paradise previously. You may want to come back to your dream location several times to experience the extremes: summer versus winter, high versus low tourist season, rainy season versus dry season, when kids are in school versus out on vacation. And don't forget about seasonal allergies.

Check out hurricane season! We had four hurricanes or tropical storms last year in just a month! That is definitely a seasonal extreme!

Another consideration is the visitation patterns of tourists and snowbirds. Do you love it during high tourist season, when there are lots of activities going on daily? How will you feel when the tourists and snowbirds go back home, and your paradise is a lot emptier of fellow expats? Does it feel lonely, or refreshing to have your favorite places to yourself again?

The key is to get a truly complete picture of your ideal location, so you can make an informed decision that you won't regret in the future.

How Long Should Your Beta Test Run?

Again, the simple answer – as long as it takes you to know what you want to do, one way or the other.

I suggest you shoot for one to two months at a minimum – long enough to go through several lifestyle cycles – grocery shopping, doing laundry, paying the rent and utilities, seeing people at monthly events, and judging the monthly ebb and flow of your life in paradise.

You want to get past the honeymoon stage and embrace the reality of your new life in paradise.

Are you constantly upset about potholes in the road, bumpy sidewalks, and stairs without handrails? How often is the electric or internet out, and how do you deal with those irritations? Do you miss having hot water in the kitchen sinks – most homes here where I live have hot water for showers only – and more rustic locations may not even offer hot water for bathing!

Are the streets too crowded, with no easy-to-find parking places?

Do you enjoy the simplicity of your new scaled-back lifestyle, with a tiny fraction of all the stuff you are used to back home? Does it feel freeing, or deprived?

Do the poverty and lack of infrastructure and inefficient processes cause you to get angry, or do you laugh it off with "ni modo", the "whatever" phrase you use when you shrug your shoulders?

How do you feel? Energized and excited and content, eager to meet new people and learn new things? Or do you feel drained by the stress of trying to communicate in broken Spanish, feel lonely and disenfranchised, bored, or resentful? This is what matters most.

My Beta Test

In the prologue, I shared a typical day from my Beta test two years ago. I came in the summer, five weeks in June and July, the steamy time of the year, when the tourists were gone, the locals were laid back, and the snowbirds had gone back to their homes to spend the summer and fall with family and friends. It was hot of course, in the high 80s every day; however, it wasn't as hot as South Texas which hits triple digits all summer long. One of the beautiful parts about living on a tropical Island is discovering that I just needed to wear a bathing suit at all times under a little shift dress, so I could hop in the water at a pool or beach two to three times a day to cool off, get some exercise, and just revel in my wonderful new life.

I rented the smallest car I could find from Enterprise near the airport, amazed by the $1 per day rental rates. Even with the extra $12 per day liability insurance, the 5 weeks cost me just around $450 – and gave me the freedom I wanted to explore and get out and about wherever and whenever I wanted. I knew I would want a car when I got here, and since the goal of the Beta Test is to replicate your lifestyle when you do move, I was happy with my tiny but reliable car. I knew how to drive a stick shift from years ago, so after a few stalls at traffic lights, I got the hang of it again. Driving in Cancun traffic was a challenge, and when I ran out of battery on my mobile phone, I had to drive around in circles looking for the car ferry – but I made it, a bit frazzled, but ready to go to my island.

I made just one night's reservation at my favorite modest hotel, knowing I could extend day by day until I found the right place to stay 'on the economy.'

I searched the local Facebook groups, and was directed to a group for long- and short-term rentals. I posted what I was looking for, and my budget, and immediately got lots of responses. I visited half a dozen places in the matter of a couple of hours. One was up too many stairs, as I had just had a full knee replacement exactly three months before, and I was being very cautious. Another was too dark. A third didn't have a patio or ocean breeze. Another was too noisy. Yet another one didn't have a kitchen.

But within the first day, I found a very nice one-bedroom condo with a huge king size bed, a tiny pool right outside the front door, good internet and TV, and a fully furnished kitchen, all on the ground floor with no steps to climb, and with parking right out the door, and I took it. I sent $1,000 by PayPal to the Canadian owner, a single man in his 40s, and moved in that same day to start my adventure in paradise.

One key takeaway from this experience is to do your Beta Test off season, while prices are cheap and there are lots of housing availabilities. I was a bit nervous not knowing in advance where I would be staying, but I learned that there are many great options, and to free myself up to the potential. I would not have had such a cavalier attitude in January, during high season, but in low season I had more options than I had imagined possible.

Networking With a Purpose

In business, I'm a master networker, and I actually teach networking skills to my college students and coaching clients. I put those skills to work and set out to learn what I needed to know in the shortest period of time possible.

I actively scheduled my day to head out every afternoon to meet and talk to people, so I visited several different expat hangouts daily to meet other recent immigrants to tap into their perspective on life in paradise.

I actively introduced myself to everyone I met and asked lots of questions. One of the secrets of networking is to realize that people love talking about themselves, and they love helping others, so you will get lots of help and support when you sincerely ask others for their insight and wisdom.

And everyone has different experiences and perspective, so often you will get conflicting information. But if you keep asking, the patterns will emerge, and you will gain a good understanding of the options available to you.

The key questions I asked everyone include:

- What made you decide to move here?
- What do you do with your time every day?
- What part of the island do you live in, and why did you choose that area?
- What's your favorite local restaurant, and what's their best dish?
- Who would you recommend for a doctor, dentist, chiropractor, massage therapist, hair stylist?
- What do you like best about living here?
- What is your biggest problem or challenge with living here?
- What's the best immigration status, and how do you get it? Pros and cons?

My biggest learning from my incessant questioning was that the best immigration option was to apply for and get my Permanent Residency Permit from the closest Mexican consulate where I lived before moving.

Everyone had a horror story of immigration problems, and the mistakes they made, and what they would do if they could do it over again. It's really valuable information, and what I learned made it so much easier for me to get it right the first time.

I learned that many people work in paradise like I do. Everyone had a bit of a different schedule, type of work arrangement, compensation plan, and time commitment, but there were many more people who were working in paradise than I had realized – I wasn't alone like I had thought.

Everyone had a different reason for moving here, but they were all important, and reinforced my decision to run away and live here where my heart beats faster. I heard the most moving reason when I asked Jeff what prompted him and his wife to move with their 5-year-old daughter and set up a craft brewery on the Island. His answer still brings tears to my eyes. He explained that he was the lead architect for an important Atlanta architecture firm, but he had nurtured the dream to open his own microbrewery for years. He said, "When the pain of not living my dream became greater than the fear of taking the leap into the unknown, I knew it was time and I had to do it."

Such intimate revelations of peoples' motivations strip away the impersonal surface impressions, and you really get to know the people you are talking with. It becomes the basis of mutual respect and friendship, and you get to peek behind the T-shirts and flipflops and get to know the fascinating, committed, interested people who surround you. And I am always amazed to learn about the skilled and talented and accomplished professionals and entrepreneurs who have chosen to live the life I dreamed about.

I knew I only had five weeks to lay the groundwork for my move, so I jumped at any and every opportunity to meet and engage with other expats so I could pick their brain – and start making friends so I wouldn't be so alone when I was ready to finally move.

I joined in lots of groups – my favorite to this day is the Sisters of Perpetual Disorder of Isla Mujeres. It's a group of about 400 expat women who live full time or part time on the island. Anywhere from 10 to 30 women meet twice a month for friendship and support. I played Rummy Cube on

Wednesdays, joined the monthly morning coffee and the mid-month evening wine social at a different member's house, and volunteered at any nonprofit event I came across.

I learned about a fundraising breakfast hosted by the Mexican Naval Officer's Wives Club and looked forward to those monthly get togethers at the Naval Club. About 100 women in total attended, and there were always several tables at the back of the room set aside for the English-speaking women, and I was able to meet a very different group of people than I met in the bars, restaurants, and beach clubs. And the lovely breakfast and social occasion cost $8, which was a donation to the Naval hospital on the island. You can't beat that.

The community is always helping others in need, and every several weeks there is a fundraiser of some kind to fund a lifesaving operation, pay a funeral bill, help a family who needs food or lodging, support a local school, or participate in a scholarship program to fund the college education of deserving local students. All these events and opportunities are posted on the different community Facebook groups, and newcomers are welcomed warmly. It's a great way to get to know people and know what is going on in your future home.

And of course, there is live music! There are a number of live music venues wherever you land, and you can always meet other active engaged people who follow their favorite performers or enjoy a special social or cultural event. And every time I met people, I asked lots of questions to get them to open up and paint a picture of what my future life in paradise may include.

Build a Network of Local and Expat Friends

I already mentioned the need to build a network of local and foreign friends, and you start now during your Beta Test. When you meet someone, offer to treat them to lunch at a favorite spot of theirs so you can get to know the area. Try to move past the superficial bar or street conversations by connecting in a meaningful way one-on-one over breakfast or lunch where you can continue gathering meaningful insights.

At my first Sisters coffee, I connected with Helena, a French woman who had moved to Isla 32 years ago, and we bonded immediately. She invited me to lunch at a tiny off-the-beaten-path eatery, and I had the chance to visit her home to see how she lived to get an idea of what a home for myself might look and feel like. She recommended a vet and a dentist, showed me the best brand of coffee to buy locally, and told me about the upcoming art market.

And the day I finally moved to my new home, she met me for lunch to welcome me to my new life in paradise! It made it so much easier to have formed bonds like that, and it all started by laying the right groundwork on my Beta Test.

We are still dear friends to this day, and I know I can count on her to help me find anything I want. When my beloved 13-year-old puppy Buddy died at home one night, she came right over to be with me, and helped me figure out what to do with his body. Friends like that are key to fitting into your life in paradise. So don't allow feeling uncomfortable or shy hold you back from building your new network to help you make a soft landing in paradise.

Five Weeks to Learn Everything I Needed to Know

I knew I had just five weeks to learn everything I needed to know to plan to move forward with my long-waited and much dreamed about move to paradise. So I set out to make sure I understood these 12 key issues which would allow me to define my next steps:

1. Legal and immigration alternatives
2. Housing options and costs
3. Communication – phone, internet, mail, TV, Netflix
4. Services – banking, credit cards, wire transfers, insurance
5. Healthcare
6. Transportation options
7. Pets and pet care
8. What to with my time and energies
9. Working in paradise

10. Cost of living

During those intense but enjoyable five weeks, I learned everything I needed to know to be completely comfortable with my planned move.

In this next chapter, I will share my learnings and takeaways to save you a lot of time, and help you structure a successful Beta Test of your own.

8. BETA TEST AHAA'S

Legal and Immigration Options

After talking with dozens of people with wildly varying experience, it became clear to me that I needed to get my permanent residency visa from the Mexican consulate where I lived before moving to Mexico. It would give me certainty for long term planning, and I had the assets I needed to meet their financial requirements, so there was no downside. Getting residency in Mexico does not affect my US citizenship in any way, or my ability to travel on a US passport, and to enter and leave the US. It just guarantees me the ability to live in Mexico for as long as I wish without limitations.

Three Immigration Categories

In a nutshell, there are three main immigration categories, and they are based on how long you plan to stay in Mexico, and how much income or assets you have. The Mexican government wants reassurance that you can pay your way and not become a burden or compete with locals for jobs.

The rules vary by year, and once you start the process, you can't change your mind and decide to submit the application in the States. A Permanent Residency visa requires the most assets or income but allows you to immediately qualify to live in Mexico forever. If you decide to apply for the Temporary Residency permit, with its lower income or asset threshold, you must go through the four-year renewal process, and you can't apply for a Permanent Residency permit until the four years are over. So I learned that for me, the best option was to start the process correctly from my local consulate, where the process can be very fast and efficient.

In perspective, it's much easier to get your Mexican visa than it is for a Mexican to get a US or Canadian permanent or temporary visa, and a lot less time and money. With the attorney and all fees combined, it cost me around $800 and three months to get my permanent residency permit. Easy peasey – when you know the ropes in advance.

Visit my website www.GrownUpsGuide.com for all the details, along with a list of immigration attorneys that may be available to help you shorten the process.

Housing Options and Costs

The next major concern I neded to explore was housing. How much would it cost to rent a comfortable home that would satisfy my needs? I visited as many people's homes as possible to check out their lifestyle, and I found lots of variations. What I did learn is that life is simpler, and you do with less overall stuff in paradise. Most people rented a furnished apartment or a whole floor of a house, so you really only need clothes and personal and work items.

Rents varied widely by season, length, location, and by negotiation. You can rent a nice one bedroom apartment for $400 a month – or $1,500. Many people happily pay $1,500 a month for a short term rental during tourist season, and feel it is a great deal. When I first heard about $400 rentals I didn't believe it. But I've seen them, and they are nice and very liveable. What I learned is that it takes a while to settle into the market, get to know people, so that you can get a referral to a great deal on housing.

Mexican homes don't look like American homes , and you may need to get used to that. Housing in different parts of Mexico may vary, and housing in major cities may be different than you will find in smaller towns or resort locations.

Here in the tropics, construction is concrete block, with tile floors – no wood or carpeting. Air conditioning is by individual room mini-splits, and no central air or heat. There's very little storage, no closets or kitchen cabinets in many homes – just poured cement shelves. You probably won't find hot water in the kitchen sink, or washers and dryers. Kitchens are smaller and sparsely furnished, as you tend to eat out much more than cook your meals at home.

But the trade offs are great. Most homes feature patios, courtyards, decks and wonderful ocean views. Houses are built with flat cement roofs which just beg to be adorned with with tables and chairs and lounges. Plants offer a riot of color and fragrance.

I decided early on that I wanted a pool, and it really limited my options as few rentals have pools. I didn't listen when people told me they didn't have pools and didn't miss them. I finally found a two-bedroom bottom floor of a house with a pool for $800 per month – in dollars with a year-long lease. I was so excited about the pool that I overlooked the dark, poorly illuminated rooms and noisy location. The American landlady turned out to be horrible, invaded my privacy by coming into my home while I was gone to "inspect things," evicted me for having houseguests over five days, and kept my rent and deposit – about $1200 in total.

In retrospect, I made the mistake of wanting to nail down my living arrangements during my Beta Test, to have a sense of certainly about where I was going to be living. Since I was moving during low season, I should have rented month to month for a couple of months to give myself time to find better deals and to choose a home that suited me better. I rushed it on my Beta Test, and was not happy with what I ended up with.

But the universe worked it out for me. It was stressful at the time – but it was a blessing in disguise.

After less than two months in my first home, I was given just three days to move out, and I acted fast. I posted that I was looking for a two bedroom apartment on several Facebook groups, and lots of people reached out to me. I spent a day visiting different homes, and settled on a much nicer, larger, bright and airy second floor two-bedroom, apartment, with a magnificent deck across the whole top of the house, Now I pay $600 per month with no contract, and have a great Mexican landlord who is really appreciative of the rent that I pay – especially as it got his whole family through the pandemic when they were all out of work.

One of my learnings is that it takes time and connections and familiarity to find your dream place. So don't stress out over it. And don't book a place sight unseen on a booking site – I've heard and seen so many horror stories! Instead, book a hotel or room to stay for a day or two, leverage your network, research Facebook groups, and rent short term to give yourself the time to ferret out the great deals. With time you will learn which part of town you want to live in, what accommodations you find acceptable, and get introduced to owners through mutual friends so you can get a great deal on a home that makes you happy. Most Mexican landlords don't require a lease, but they will charge a one-month deposit for a multi-month rental, which gives you the flexibility to move when you find just the perfect home. So remember, it's not forever, just for today.

Communication – Phone, Internet, Netflix

For me, inexpensive effective communication with my clients is critical to keeping my business running, so I searched out options for great high speed Wi-Fi and mobile phone service. Communication services can vary dramatically by region, so it's a good practice to ask other expats, or post a querry on the local Facebook groups in your dream location. Key options to explore include:

Keep Your US or Canadian Mobile Service

My mobile phone carrier in the States is AT&T, and they offer an international plan for just another $5 per month that gives unlimited phone and data – a steal. Other friends report that TMobile, Sprint, Verizon, and Google Fi offer great inexpensive plans – but the secret is that you must set up the correct plan in advance. If you don't, you can get hit with hundreds or even thousands of dollars of long distance and international roaming charges in just a few days.

Paul, a Canadian, went to his local Walmart and set up an international plan for his Bell Canada phone. Just one day into a 30 day trip, he got a message that he had been charged $280 in international roaming charges, and his phone service was cut off for the whole month! When he got back and showed them the signed contract, they said – oops – sorry, we made an error – and they did not give him his money back. So make sure you do your research in advance, and document it.

Get a Local Mobile Phone

Once you get settled into paradise, you might decide to change from a US or Canadian phone number to a local number. Or you might decide to have a second local phone with a local phone number.   There are a lot of benefits, including accessing your bank's mobile app, and you can take advantage of incredibly inexpensive local mobile phone services for $5 or $10 per month. The key local carriers in Mexico are Telcel, Movistar, AT&T, and Virgin Mobile. You can find service providers at malls and grocery stores and stand-alone phone stores as well, where you can buy phones and SIM cards, choose your service provider and plan, and buy airtime.

Most people buy air time or a prepaid card, rather than have a monthly credit account – since they don't recognize your US credit report. And you can repurpose a US phone by changing the SIM card if you can get it unlocked, either by buying it without a phone service plan, or having it hacked locally.

There is a great article that discusses mobile phone options in Mexico and you can read it on my website. Like anything, especially here in Mexico, terms and conditions and offerings may change at any time, so check right before you travel to make sure you have up-to-date information.

Instant Messaging Options

In the States, we use free text messaging provided by our mobile phone company to communicate - but not in Mexico! The mobile companies at one time charged expensive fees for SMS chat services, so in many developing countries, they use free internet-based chat services instead.

Here everyone uses WhatsApp, which is an option for calling when you create a contact on your phone. Another option is Facebook Messenger, which is also a free service. And lots of people are moving to Telegram with privacy and censoring concerns. The advantage of all of these is you can access the platforms on both your phone and your laptop, while you can't access mobile phone chat on your computer. You can also integrate business calls and look up businesses on Messenger which makes it easier to contact people you don't have in your phone book. And WhatsApp is adding business accounts as well as personal accounts. The disadvantage is that you have to have a Wi-fi connection, or they won't work. And don't forget Zoom, which I use all the time, and Skype, both free app services for a basic plan., and which work off cellular data so you don't need to be connected to Wi-Fi to access them. Don't fight it – download all the apps to your phone and laptop to hit the ground running.

Google Voice For Toll Free Numbers

You cannot dial many US or Canadian toll-free numbers from your Mexican phone, or even from your US phone in Mexico – which is a major hassle. But there is a way – and it's free. Get a Google Voice account, which assigns you a US virtual phone number, and allows you to access its services from both your phone and computer. It syncs to your phone's address book to access all your contacts, even on a laptop. It only works for US phone numbers at this time, and it appears you need to set it up while you are in the US. Since your airlines, banks, credit cards, hotels, and more generally provide only toll-free numbers, this is a life saver to make sure you stay in touch.

High Speed Internet

Again, services vary by region, and you should ask the expat community for suggestions and recommendations of reliable service where you plan to live. I battled to get this fine-tuned and hope I can save you the headaches I experienced.

Many rentals will offer free internet services, but the bandwidth may be too low to meet your needs.

Internet services are sold by bandwidth, with the 'standard' high speed bandwidth here being 20 or 30 MB. What they don't tell you is that this is the download speed – like for watching Netflix. The upload speed is dramatically slower – unless you know to specify a higher speed. I battled with one highly recommended internet service, with poor customer service, and experienced Zoom calls that dropped constantly, long file download times, and impossible file uploads, and the like. They kept telling me it wasn't their service, but that my laptop was defective.

In desperation, I switched services, and by chance learned that I had to order synchronous service – 30 MB download AND 30 MB upload – and my problem was fixed. It was more expensive, and I now pay about $87 per month for the service, but it works! And the company offers excellent customer service, with 24/7 live chat, and technicians that arrive on their motorcycles in half an hour to troubleshoot problems. I learned during the process that you can use free apps like SpeedTest to diagnose your internet speed, and that is what I used to prove that I wasn't getting the right service and insisted that they fix it – which they did.

Get a US URL

When you use your phone and computer, many applications will use geolocation to personalize communication – and they will automatically switch you over to serving content in the local language. That means you may have a hard time accessing your US or Canadian sites and content in English. For example, you may be defaulted to local Netflix, Amazon, and Walmart sites in Spanish and in pesos, on both your computer and phone. Bank of America will not let me make mobile deposits on my phone because they detect that I am physically out of the country. Some local internet providers can assign you a US URL, which solves that problem - the web will see a Houston or Miami URL, rather than a Mexican one. This also prevents lots of security checks – "We've identified a log in from a foreign location – was this you?"

TV Station Options

You will have access to local broadcast stations, and with high-speed internet, you may have options to access cable programs. Many Mexican homes have access to Netflix – with Spanish language programs. But you can watch all your favorite TV shows and movies when you log onto a US internet provider that offers mobile services. Just use your US service, or get login information from a friend or family member that will allow you to access their account, and you will have access to all your multimedia offerings. You can have your own profile set up on Netflix and it's just like being back home.

Most TVs here are Smart TVs and you can get YouTube, Amazon Music and Videos, Hulu, and other viewing apps that will deliver you the media you want in your own language. My internet provider recommended that I get an Amazon Firestick for quick access to all my media on my TV, and it works seamlessly with the single click of a button.

Get a VPN – Virtual Private Network

If you travel and find spotty internet, you can try to get better service through subscription to a VPN, which will connect you with the nearest high speed internet access point. I've used Express VPN for several years. It helped a lot when traveling, when I was unable to access any public Wi-Fi, and it was better than nothing, because internet access when roaming in remote areas can be a real challenge. Now I used it to provide a US URL so I can access programs in English on services like Netflix, Amazon Prime TV and Music, YouTube TV, and even US broadcast and cable channels – all my favorites from home.

Tech Support

What do you do when you have computer problems in paradise? If you have a Best Buy Total Protection 24/7 Service plan, you can get online remote customer service, diagnostics and debugging day or night just like you were back home from US technicians. The cost is around $200 per year, and I've had my plan for many years and couldn't live without it. Find out more including the link to subscribe to the service on my website.

Best Buy, Office Depot, Office Max and Apple all have local stores in Mexico where you can access tech products, services, and repairs, often at costs that are less than in the US. And ask around and you should be able to find local individuals and companies who can provide tech support for incredibly low rates.

I discovered that there is a whole Technology Mall, which is a wing of a shopping mall in Cancun (as well as one in Merida) where there are three floors of tech resources. The bottom floor provides sales of every kind of new and sometimes used technology products. The second floor has dozens of repair kiosks which will instantly fix your phone or laptop for peanuts. My iPhone screen broke – twice – and a full repair with original Apple screen costs less than $100 and took 45 minutes. And the third floor is for video gamers and online gaming resources. When I discovered this, I felt like a kid in a candy store, and I share videos of the mall at my YouTube channel and Facebook page.

The key point is that there are many more technology resources available overseas than you may have imagined, so don't be fearful about not having them available. You just have to be resourceful in finding them.

In summary, the local and expatriate communities are keys to accessing these valuable resources, and it's reassuring to know that you are not in a technology desert you may have feared. Just reach out for help on Facebook groups and in person to find what your need to know. And always check the Resource section of my website for up-to-the-minute information and valuable resources and links.

Money and Banking

It's critical to be able to access your money when and where you need it, and you should use your Beta Test to research available services in advance to avoid exhorbitant fees or being stranded without access to your funds.

Currency Exchange

You can exchange your dollars for local currency at your US or Canadian bank before departing on your trip, and get a good rate.

However, if you plan to exchange a large amount, you may have to advise the bank in advance to make sure they have the funds on hand.

When exchanging dollars at local banks and money changers, make sure you are getting the best rate, as they vary greatly. You will be required by the Mexican government to present your valid passport to exchange dollars to pesos at the bank – it's an effort to stop money laundering. The teller will count out the money in front of you, but make sure you recount it, as some tellers are known for shortchanging you with a sleight of hand.

ATM Machines

You can generally access your money through a bank account debit card or credit card at an ATM machine, and they are freely available in most cities and towns. The local ATM operator may charge $1 – 2 fee locally, but check with your bank or card issuer to find out if there is a per-transaction fee that can rack up big charges fast. Most ATM machines will deliver funds only in the local currency, so you will not have funds available in dollars while traveling.

Opening a Mexican Bank Account

I asked around, and I found a small Mexican bank that allowed me to open a bank account without being a legal resident. I had to show a local address, as evidenced by an electric bill with the address, and a letter from my landlord saying I was renting, or a copy of a lease. This makes life so much easier! I can easily and quickly wire myself funds from my US bank account, and it takes just one day to arrive. And when I wire funds to myself from my Bank of America account, they don' t even charge me a wire transfer fee or commission! Plus I get at least a 5% higher exchange rate than I would using an ATM card at the bank.

I use my Mexican ATM card for all purchases in Mexico, and don't get charged a transaction fee. They send email notifications of all transactions, so I can track any use of my card or account. I also learned that I can only access my online banking account using my laptop computer or a a Mexican mobile phone – good to know!

And my Mexican bank offers lots of other services – including issuing my auto insurance policy on the spot – who would have guessed?

When I visted my friend Sue in Ajijic in the Lake Chapala area, the huge expatriate center there hosted a local English-speaking banker several hours a day to sign up new account holders, and answer questions about banking options.

I am sure there are many smaller or local banks that will offer the same service where you plan to visit and live – ask around for recommendations.

Credit Cards

Before you embark on your Beta Test, advise all your credit cards that you will be traveling out of the country, and the dates, to prevent security concerns from blocking access. Some bank accounts and credit cards allow you to do this online or on a mobile app; in other cases, it might be easier just to call the customer service number on the card to advise them of your travel dates and details.

While you are doing that, make sure you set up autopay of the minimum balance on all your credit cards or payment obligations. When I set off on my Beta Test, I knew I would be gone for four to six weeks, so I called every single card to set up autopay. I have several Capital One cards, so with one call I was able to set up auto pay on all of them. Imagine how shocked I was when I got notice on my credit app that my credit score had dropped 47 points in one day! I had just returned from my Beta Test, and guess what? The Capital One customer service rep had entered a wrong digit for the bank routing number on one card, and as it cycled through two monthly cycles, the ridiculously low minimum payment of $16 was not made for two billing cycles in a row, and I was flagged for a delinquent account. I immediately called Capital One customer service, got lots of apologies and all the late fees and charges waived, and my account was reinstated with them. But the damage was done. The default hit all the credit bureaus, and Capital One was unable to correct the default. I protested to all the credit reporting organizations, to no avail. To this day, I am still battling the credit issue, and it will take several more years before the "default" will age out of my credit report.

Not only that, but the "default" caused all my other credit cards to reevaluate my credit worthiness, which resulted in several of them dramatically lowering my credit limit. My main Chase Southwest Airlines credit card, which I used to earn points for travel, lowered my credit limit from $4,000 to $400! That means that my same balance became a higher percentage of my credit line usage, so that resulted in a further reduction in my credit score as card after card reduced my credit availability. What a mess! Don't let this happen to you. Set up autopay well in advance so you don't miss a payment.

Setting Up Digital Mail Service

It is useless to use Mexican mail service to do just about anything! It can take two to four months to get a Christmas card delivered – I got one in March! And I paid a $35 rush international shipping fee for a book more than five months ago – and to this day have never received it.

Perhaps you have family members who will diligently open all your mail, scan and file important documents, and update you frequently on correspondence received, and you don't have anything you want to keep private from them. If so, then perhaps they will handle your mail for you.

For the rest of us, you will be well served to get a virtual mailbox service to serve as a permanent address, extablish your residency in a low- or no-tax state, and handle all your mail and package delivery needs.

There are a number of digital mail service providers to choose from, and most provide similar services:

- A permanent street address (not a PO Box address)

- Mail and package reception and storage until pickup, or forwarding services

- Mail scanning, archiving, shredding, forwarding and even check deposits

- Archive scanned email amd document images for a long period of time

- Access your password-protected mailbox from either a computer or your phone app.

Many digital mail services are provided by shared workspace companies, as part of their suite of services. Pricing ranges from $6.99 a month to $59 per month, so check pricing carfully. I contracted mine through the shared workspace company of a friend, and am glad I was able to solve the mail issue so quickly and easily. For an updated list of recommended digital mailbox vendors, visit my website.

State Income Tax Implications

When you move overseas, your state may decide to assess you with State Income Tax regardless of the Federal Government's $100,000 Foreign Earned Income Deduction. Therefore, before you move overseas, you will want to establish your legal and physical domicile in a state with no state income tax -like Texas or Florida. That's another reason a virtual mailbox can be so important, because it gives you a physical street address you can claim as your permanent address. Send change of address notifications to everyone and every business, including the IRS, Social Security, Medicare, your banks and credit cards, etc. Make sure you order a new drivers license, and a new voter registration card to be sent to your new address. Hopefully, you can have a friend or relative pickup your packages and credit cards, etc. periodically to avoid paying storage fees. This one move alone can save you tens of thousands of dollars in state income taxes!

Your Change of Address Takes Time – So Start Today

When you move, it may take many months to make sure all your mail is changed over to your new virtual mail box address, so start today sending in change of address notifications. When you do move, you can forward your mail to the new address – and trust me, you will be amazed at the number of mail items that still are addressed to your prior address.

You will also have many online apps and programs that automatically store your physical address – including Amazon, shopping apps, any service or product you buy online, anywhere that you have used a credit card or physical address in the past - and your old address may pop up for years. You may want to go to your password managers and delete all old addresses because they won't do it automatically, no matter how many times you enter your new mailing address. Be aware that it may take years – start now so it's one less thing to do when you do start your move to paradise.

Healthcare and Medical Access

In Chapter 5, we discussed medical care options, so I just want to summarize key learnings you should seek to gather during your Beta Test:

Get Referrals

Ask for referrals from everyone you know for medical professionals – doctors, dentists, specialists, plastic surgeons, physical therapists, med spas, massage therapists, chiropractors, opthamologists, and any other health care professionals you might need. If you post in community Facebook groups, you should receive lots of wholehearted recommendations.

Schedule a Meet and Greet Appointment

Schedule a get acquainted visit to meet and greet the professional, discuss your needs, perhaps set up a preliminary file, and review medications you take to decide if you are better served to buy them in the US or Canada, or source them locally. You may get a free consultation, or pay a small office visit fee of about $25. For chiropractors and massage therapists, you can schedule your first session, and enjoy it!

Medical Emergencies and Hospitals

Ask your local doctor how they handle medical emergencies – is there a local hospital, or will you be taken to a medical center in a larger city? Ask about the hospital options available, and ask for recommended hosptials or medical clinics. How will you be transferred to the larger medical facility if needed? Make sure you understand the payment process, as you may be required to pay for hospitalization before you are admitted. They generally won't bill you or insurance; you will probably have to pay cash in advance, and you may want to explore having a credit card on hand to use just for medical emergencies. My friend Eve had emergency gall bladder removal, and the hospital personnel ran along side her gurney heading to the operating room with a mobile credit card terminal to process the payment then and there!

On a brighter note, I just had two major medical emergencies – a ruptured appendix, and a tumor in an enlarged kidney - and had to have surgery to remove them both just a few weeks apart. My doctor arranged advanced approval of insurance coverage as an emergency with my AARP Medicare Complete Advantage Plan, I signed a bunch of papers in English in the hospital, and the complete process was covered 100% by insurance. I just paid tips to the ambulance attendants and boat captain who ferried me across the Bay of Cancun at midnight in a hospital ambulance boat. I have posted videos on my Facebook page to document and share the adventure.

Medical Insurance and Medevac Plans

You may want to consider a private medical insurance plan or emergency medevac evacuation insurance during your Beta Test and later when you move to your new home in paradise. I learned that you can buy long term policies, or write a six-month emergency evacuation plan that suits your needs for relatively low costs. But many plans require you to apply for coverage and do medical screening in advance from the States and won't allow enrollment while overseas. You can also find international health insurance plans that will provide coverage overseas for a fraction of the cost of a US medical insurance plan. Go to my website or an updated list of recommended programs that might suit your needs.

Explore Options for Medicare Insurance Coverage

Generally, Medicare will not cover any services when you are traveling or living overseas. However, I discovered that you may be able to get some form of coverage from either a MediGap plan, or a Medicare Advantage provider. I have AARP Medicare Complete from Secure Horizons, and I learned that they would reimburse me a portion of any emergency care I would receive in a hospital overseas. They will not pay for any routine visits, which are very inexpensive here, just emergency care. Again, check up to date information on my website www.GrownUpsGuide.com.

Get Your Current Medical Files You Can Access Overseas

Before traveling or moving, you may want to ask your doctors and dentists to provide digital files of recent treatments, lab results, medications, XRays or MRIs, etc, so you can access them from your new home. Most doctors offices today have password-protected online housing of your medical data, so make sure you have access to it before you head out on your new adventure.

Transportation Options

There are lots of local transportation options, from walking, taking the bus for under $1, or taking a taxi just about anywhere on the island for $3 or less. Bigger cities offer Uber and Lyft, while smaller markets will provide inexpensive taxi service. I knew I wanted to have my own vehicle for indepence, so I explored the local options:

Golf Carts

Many expats choose golf carts – and I long said that my next car would be a golf cart. During my Beta Test, I discovered that they are a lot of fun when you are a tourist, but a maintenance headache when you own one.

And here at least, they are ridiculously expensive. A 20-year-old used golf cart with a valid tag can easily cost $5,000 – not so much for the vehicle itself, but for the scarce tag. The powerful taxi union twisted the arm of the local government to not issue any more permits, creating artificial scarcity, and driving prices through the roof. And everyone talks about their golf cart breaking down, and the hassle of constant repairs. Plus in the winter and rainy season, when the tourists have long gone, it is nasty to drive an open vehicle in the driving rain. They are, however, a lot of fun to drive on a vacation.

Motor Scooters

There are literally thousands of motor scooters anywhere you go in Mexico, and it is the preferred mode of transportation for the local residents, who often pack a family of 4 onto a beat up old moto, thankful they don't have to walk everywhere. A number of expats choose motos, and you can buy one brand new in the supermarket for under $1,000!

Used motos can cost as low as $300 or $400 – and are easy to resell. I know several people who live on 40+-foot boats, and they bring their moto with them for local transportation whenever they dock.

I personally would never consider a moto, since I am older and have had a knee replacement, and know that even a tiny tumble could jeapordize my mobility. But it's definitely an option for many people who love the ability to zip into town and find a parking space anywhere fast. I have several female friends that drive motos and they swear by them. And of course many men prefer a moto over a golf cart.

Cars

I knew that I wanted to have a car of my own, and during my Beta Test, I rented the smallest car I could find from Enterprise for just $1 per day – plus $12 per day of liability insurance. It fit my needs perfectly, so I knew going forward that I would want to buy my own car. But I learned that life in Paradise is hard on cars, and you can bet on lots of bumps and scrapes as you park creatively, drive up on curbs for parking, or park in dirt lots near the beach, or just park on narrow streets where the huge beer or bottled water transportaion trucks can sideswipe your car or knock off your side mirror.

I was very careful with my rental car to avoid damage, but it convinced me I wanted a very small older car when I got settled in. If you'd like to learn more about my car buying adventure when I did move to paradise, you can find all the details in my next book The Runaway Roadmap – Your Step-by-step Guide to Escape to Paradise. You will also learn lots of tips to avoid making a mistake.

Beta Test – Pass or Fail?

During my five-week Beta Test, I learned a lot. And it was enough to assure me that my dream to move to Paradise was not just feasible, but achievable, and it would give me what I was looking for in life. I was able to prove to myself that my dream could become a reality. Finally, I found the opportunity to combine my passion for the beach life with the reality of working in Paradise to support myself, and that I could live richly on a small budget.

My Beta Test gave me the freedom to move from dreaming to planning – creating a firm vision for my future and putting together the plan to make it happen.

And your Beta Test can do the same for you!

So now we move into the next phase – crafting the plan of transformation.

And it starts with understanding the money – how much money and what assets do you have now, what is your transferrable income flow, how much will it cost to live your dream lifestyle, and can you earn what you need to make the leap to freedom.

Let's go through the process together in the next chapter.

9. SO HOW MUCH WILL IT COST YOU TO LIVE IN PARADISE?

Most people find that living in Mexico, most Latin American countries, and other developing parts of the world allows you to live for half the cost of living in the US or Canada – or less. And many find they can even live well on their modest Social Security check alone!

There are a number of reasons for that huge savings:

- Rents are less than half of what you would pay in the US or Canada
- The actual cost of purchasing goods and services is less
- Medical care and insurance are dramatically less
- Personal services are ridiculously low, due to local wages of around $5 per day!
- You require less "stuff" when you change your lifestyle

You hopefully will find your life simpler, less cluttered, and less burdensome when you escape to paradise. It's not just the process of downsizing that you do before you move. It's also that you require less of just about everything when you move to paradise. A smaller home. No car, or an older inexpensive vehicle, or a scooter. No commuting expenses. No downtown parking garage expense. No meals out on an hour lunch break before dashing back to the office. No expensive business suits or professional attire. No overpriced Starbucks coffees to keep you awake during your commute. No vending machine sodas or treats.   Less home maintenance. Not keeping up with the Joneses. Fewer furnishings, especially if you rent.

Simpler clothing needs. Fewer bells and whistles. Cheap medicine. And so much more.

You also benefit from incredibly inexpensive services for just about everything: $5 house cleaning or gardening, $12 manicures and pedicures, $20 haircuts and colors, $25 massages, $25 chiropractic or doctors' appointments, inexpensive dentistry, cheap taxi service, almost free sewing repairs and any labor-intensive services.

My Living Expenses in Paradise

I was amazed at how little it costs me to live in paradise, and I am fascinated that every month I find new ways to whittle away expenses as I get deeper and deeper connected into the fabric of local life. At this point, a bit less than two years after moving to Paradise, it costs me less than $1,500 per month to live well and richly. These are my costs:

My total housing cost is under $1,000 a month versus more than $2,900 a month for my rented house in the States. I pay around $600 a month for my 1,100 SF fully furnished 2-bedroom apartment with a huge roof top patio. My rent is higher than other parts of Mexico because I live in a much sought-after beach resort. My rent includes water and gas. In Cancun and smaller towns, you could get the same home for $300 - $400 a month. I have many friends who enjoy smaller fully furnished one-bedroom apartments with a small balcony for $400 per month. I chose a two-bedroom home because I expected to have lots of guests – and I wanted it to be very comfortable for us all. If I needed to cut expenses, I could get a roommate, and reduce my housing expenses by half to less than $500, which becomes incredibly affordable.

My electric bill runs between $35 and $150 per month, depending on the season. In the lovely temperate winter and spring, I don't use air conditioning, and have the doors and windows wide open to enjoy the soothing ocean breeze. In the summer, the weather is hot (85 – 90 degrees) and steamy with high humidity, so I run the air conditioning in my bedroom and office pretty much all day and night, and sometimes in the rest of the house if I will be cooking or entertaining.

Internet - I have upgraded my internet for a full 30 MB of upload and download so I can host webinars and Zoom calls, and pay $80 per month, vs. my $250 US cable bill with hundreds of TV channels. I access cable TV from the States via a remote login from a friend's cable company, and access Netflix and Hulu through the internet on a smart TV.

Housecleaning - My neighbor lady cleans my house twice a week for $5 per cleaning, versus $100 per cleaning I paid in Texas each week. My home is smaller, and has less stuff to clean around, and has tile floors which are easy to clean. She's in and out generally in less than 2 hours, and lately I've been leaving my key with her so she can clean if I'm not at home when her hubby comes from his job and is able to watch the two small children. Sometimes I think she just enjoys the peace and quiet of my house – along with the air conditioning!

Water – In my current home, the water is included. In a different house where I lived, the monthly water bill was 150 pesos – about $7 a month. Everyone here drinks bottled water, and I have the deliverymen from the water truck bring the big five-gallon bottles up the steps, and put them in the dispenser, and with a generous tip, it comes out to under $2.50 per bottle (called a garrafón) once a week.

Laundry – Few people here in Mexico have washers and dryers, and either hand wash or use a local laundry service. I hand wash my undies, nighties, and my everyday lightweight sleeveless dresses and blouses and slacks. I take sheets, pillowcases, towels, throw rugs and cleaning rags to the local laundry (lavandería), where I pay less than

$4 for a full load of laundry, washed, dried, folded and packaged into large plastic bags.

Cleaning Products and Miscellaneous Expenses – I spend less than $20 per month for all my cleaning products, which I buy at the local grocery store. If I'm out of something, my cleaning lady will run to the store around the corner to pick up a bottle of Fabuloso or bleach, or whatever, for less than $1.

My Groceries And Meals are maybe half of what I would spend in the States, $400 to $500 monthly, versus a $1,000 back home, where I ate a lot of fast food and processed food. I cooked at home during the pandemic lockdown, but generally go out once a day for dinner, and spend around $10 - $15 for a good meal at a restaurant or beach club. I don't drink a lot and prefer a glass of wine or a mimosa at home rather than expensive drinks at a bar or restaurant, so I generally end up drinking sparkling water with meals. I try to eat just one meal a day, sometimes two, so if I eat a meal at home, it is a quick quesadilla for lunch, or a steak, shrimp or lobster dinner I cook at home in the evening.

My Personal Care Expenses again are less than half of what I spent before coming here. A manicure or pedicure costs $12, a haircut and style maybe $12 - $15. I pamper myself with a weekly 2-hour full body massage on the terrace under the moon for $45 – and I deserve it! Pet grooming for the dog is $20 vs $55 in the States.

Medical Expenses are a fraction of what it costs in the US as well. I am fortunate in that I have a Medicare Complete Advantage Plan, which provides free or low-cost US doctors' visits and mail order prescription meds in the US. Now thanks to Covid, I can access my US doctor any time on a telemedicine video call, the exact same way I would if I were back in the States. I order my prescription medications in 90-day quantities and arrange to have them sent to a friend who is coming down to visit within the next month or so.

I have a standing chiropractic adjustment every two weeks for 500 pesos – around $23, and I pay the same amount to see the leading English-speaking physicians Dr. Greta or Dr. Salas in their offices. They do offer home visits if needed for a small upcharge, but not much. You don't need a doctors' prescription to buy most medicines in a local pharmacy, and drug costs again are a fraction of US prices. Dental cleanings and fillings and other services are again a tiny percentage of US prices, so all in all, I budget less than $100 per month for medical and dental care.

Transportation expenses are also at a minimum. In the States, I commuted 38 miles each way to teach at Texas A&M University weekly, which costs $40 per week or $160 a month, and I had to pay an annual $100 fee to park on campus. And I lived in the suburbs, so I never walked anywhere. My auto expenses were $60 a week for gas, more for everyday mileage and wear and tear, plus auto maintenance, parking, tolls, etc.

Here in paradise, there are lots of local transportation options, from walking, taking the bus for under $1, or taking a taxi just about anywhere for $3.

I wanted the independence of having my own car, so I sold my beautiful Chrysler Sebring convertible, which I loved, and paid $1,750 to buy a 2005 little Chevy (that's the model name), with air conditioning and a radio, but without power steering or automatic transmission, which is my run-around beach buggy. My insurance is less than $300 per year, or about $25 a month, a fraction of what I paid back in the States. Gasoline is more expensive per gallon than in many parts of the US, and I buy 500 pesos of gas twice a month, for around $50 - $75 per month.

Car maintenance is incredibly cheap. A truck knocked off my driver's side mirror, and it cost me $15 to have it reattached by a local mechanic. My auto registration is less than $25 per year, and parking fines (of which I have gotten 3 so far) come out to about $35 each. So I spend under $100 a month on transportation versus more than $350 a month in the States.

Other expenses – I maintain a virtual office in Texas which gives me digital mailbox services, for about $500 per year. I am looking into buying an expatriate medical emergency evacuation plan for about $750 for a year but haven't moved forward with it yet – as you have to be back in the States to write the policy. I also hedged my bets when I moved by keeping a room in a girlfriend's apartment, and chipping in $400 per month towards the rent. If I decide I don't need that security blanket and can find another way to store or deal with my treasures, I can reduce or eliminate that expense.

Summary – All in all, even with the extra expenses, my living costs are around $2,100 per month, compared to $5,000 per month in the States. That's a whopping big reduction of 58% over what it cost me to live in San Antonio, which is one of the lower costs US markets. Plus, if I chose to share the rent of my apartment with a roommate, it would be down around $1,700 per month, even with luxuries like weekly massages, mani-pedis, and lots of meals out. And without the apartment back in the States, I'd be looking at around $1,300 per month. This lifestyle is affordable to almost anyone on Social Security or a retirement plan. And that is without the other side of the equation – earning money while living in paradise.

Create Your Own Monthly Cost of Living Budget

You can easily create your own Cost of Living Analysis starting with these numbers, and then fine tune them to reflect your different lifestyle choices. Maybe you want a larger or more luxurious home with a pool, or opt to live in a smaller one-bedroom apartment for now. Whatever your variables, you can start with the cost-of-living calculator which you can find at my websi8te www.GrownUpsGuide.com. Take the time right now to create a rough plan to help you figure out just how doable this is.

The key message it that YOU can live in paradise for a fraction of what you would spend in the States or Canada – probably on your Social Security check alone. This is truly feasible!

Let's keep building out your financial plan to make sure we don't face any nasty surprises.

Create Your Cash Flow Analysis

Once you have a good idea of your current and projected living expenses, you can create a cash flow analysis. You can use the template you will find on my website, or just write it down on a piece of blank paper.

Draw a line down the middle of a sheet of paper. On one side, write down all your monthly expenses – rent or mortgage, property taxes, home and auto insurance premiums, utilities, medical insurance, minimum credit card payments, payments on any other liabilities. Analyze your bank account and credit card bills to make sure you don't forget things like monthly subscriptions, computer and mobile phone expenses, pest control or homeowner's association fees, memberships, donations, customary tithing or support of your church, and anything else you spend money on. That will be your expense budget.

On the other side of the paper, write down all your income – salary from your job, consulting income, freelance work, Social Security and pension income, alimony or child support, loan repayments, royalties, dividends, and more.

If your expenses are greater than your income, start making adjustments. Cut your monthly expenses or take steps to generate additional income. When the two balance, or you have more income than expenses, you are free to initiate your move to paradise.

Create your Balance Sheet

Your Cash Flow plan is just one part of the financial plan that will allow you to move to paradise on your own terms. You should also create your Balance Sheet, listing all your financial assets on the left side of a sheet, and your liabilities on the right side.

Your assets will include cash in bank, investments, your retirement funds, your 401K, IRA, stocks, bonds, annuities, and things that you can readily turn into cash.

Calculate the realistic market value of your house, less the mortgage and needed improvements, and deduct 10% of the market value of your house to cover sales commissions and fees when you sell it, to determine the value of what is generally your biggest asset. If you have other real estate, do the same.

Likewise, get a realistic idea of the resale value of your car or any other vehicles (RV, boat, motorcycle, plane, etc.), less the balance of payments due, to list that in the asset column.

In the liabilities column, list credit card debt, notes payable, personal loans, student loans, and anything else that you owe. Don't list your mortgage if you've inputted it into calculating the net value of your home when you sell it. Subtract the liabilities from the assets to determine your net worth. Hopefully you will have a healthy positive balance of more assets than liabilities.

Plan to Turn Both Assets and Liabilities into Cash

Identify any assets that you have that will no longer meet your needs when you decide to run away to live in paradise and start to sell them to convert them into cash, which you will need. This can include cars or vehicles, a boat, RV, ATV, or other fun vehicles. You can sell the lake cottage, your vacation home, the duplex you bought for the kids to live in while they were away at college, undeveloped real estate – you get the picture. Home furnishings are hard to sell, and we will deal with them in Chapter 14, but for now, inventory all the assets you don't need and take action to turn them into cash, either as a lump sum, or an ongoing revenue stream.

Likewise, you should be evaluating your liabilities, and seek ways to convert them to assets. That could include renting out that duplex or converting it into a business. If you own a business than can provide cash flow, make sure that you either have someone totally reliable to run it for you, or that you structure the business so you can manage it at a distance, and not have to be hands on, or it will defeat the purpose and may prevent you from running away from home.

Are You Ready?

Now that you've done these financial exercises, you should be in a good place to figure out how much more income you will need to escape to your paradise now. It will take time to make these financial transformations, so start early to be ready to move when the opportunity presents itself.

Now let's proceed on to the next big step in your plan to escape to freedom – figuring out how to make money to support yourself while living in paradise.

10. RUN AWAY EARLIER THAN YOU EVER THOUGHT POSSIBLE

You may have thought you needed to work until you were 65 or 70 before you could retire to be able to move to paradise.

Well, not anymore!

Today you can run away from home much earlier than you ever dreamed possible – and you have many options and choices that can accelerate your move to freedom.

Most people work until they think they can afford to retire before they plan to move to paradise.

I suggest that you look at the choice differently. Ask yourself – What do I need to do to be able to run away to live in paradise today?

The logical option is to reduce your expenses to a lifestyle that you can support in your dream location, and at the same time find flexible remote income to be able to embrace your desired lifestyle now.

Work from Home - Thanks to the Coronavirus Pandemic!

The Covid-19 pandemic has changed our lives in so many ways. This is one of the good ways! And it actually makes running away from home easier than you ever thought possible.

Perhaps the most positive result of this global crisis will be the permanent trend to working from home. It's a genie that probably will never go back into the bottle.

Employers have resisted this trend for years, but the crisis has forced the mass exodus of legions of employees from office buildings to working from home. And it's working. Once the kids go back to school, lots of folks will find that they enjoy it, and are very productive.

And when employers realize that they can save $18,300 per employee EACH YEAR in office expenses, they should soon embrace the trend as they realize the tradeoff between the control of employees in the office versus reduced costs and improved employee job productivity and satisfaction.

This trend is being pioneered by the big tech companies, which have already announced that they will maintain work from home options well into the future. Other employers are following suit, to be able to maintain a competitive advantage in the work force.

Basically, any job that can be done in a cubicle on a laptop or phone can be done from the comfort of your own home. So, take advantage of it!

Who Defines Where "Home" Is?

Today, more than half of the US work force is working from home. So who defines where "Home" is? You may discover that you can work from a home office a bit further away than your coworkers, like 2,000 miles away instead of 20 miles away. The person on the other end of the phone or camera won't be able to tell the difference.

I work as a career coach, marketing consultant, and author from my home in Isla Mujeres. I enjoy life in a beautiful peaceful location, while I'm able to engage with customers and business associates anywhere in the world by phone and internet. And so can you.

You don't have to work for 40 or 50 years in the States and then retire in your sixties and seventies and eighties to start to live a life of joy

Instead, start examining ways that you can work remotely from your little piece of paradise, whether it's on a white sandy beach here in Mexico, or another place that makes you happy.

You may even want to change jobs or careers to be able to work remotely, but you now have options you never even dreamed possible just a few months ago.

By thinking creatively about your job, career and future, you can find a way to run away from home to live in paradise much earlier than you ever imagined possible.

You can have an active, proactive, wonderful career as long as you use today's digital and online resources and tap into the infrastructure of technology that's available out there today.

There are many ways you can live and work effectively here in paradise to achieve your goals. Let's explore some of the most significant ones.

Bring Your Corporate Job with You

I know many people who work at their corporate jobs, but while enjoying a rich life in paradise. This is just a snapshot of a few of them.

Allison works in inside sales and customer service for a book publisher and reseller. She works most mornings, and by 4 p.m. she joins her husband at a beach bar he manages.

Cathy works as a copywriter in a Dallas ad agency, logging in to work at 9 a.m., and logging out at 5 p.m. Monday through Friday to head to the beach for the rest of the afternoon.

Karen is a financial planner and cash manager for a major grocery store chain in the US. Like many office dwellers, she was sent to work from her home office at the beginning of the pandemic, and said "Why not go back to my vacation spot here in Mexico to work online?" Her employer doesn't even know she's not in the States anymore. And she knows she can hop on a plane and be back in less than a day if she needs to show up at the corporate headquarters.

Michelle is a financial planner for a brokerage firm. She takes care of customers four to six hours a day, working from her home office overlooking the Bay of Cancun, and taking a dip in the crystal-clear water of her pool just feet from her office window during lunch hour or after she wraps up for the day.

Julie is a mortgage loan broker and processes all the paperwork remotely to support a four-person real estate brokerage firm. She worked out of her home office before the pandemic, and now sees no reason to stay in the States since everything she does is online.

Work for Your Own US-Based Business in Paradise

A number of other friends are self-employed, running their own businesses from paradise.

Karen has a grant writing business based in Colorado, and she supports her customers online, while her son manages much of the day-to-day administrative work back home. She travels back to the States every two months or so for a week or two for scheduled meetings, and then heads back to her island to enjoy life.

Keesha is a mental health counselor and therapist, and she works totally online by video therapy sessions with clients. She has established office hours Monday through Saturday and works around six hours a day from the third bedroom of her house, with no office rental expenses. Talk about a win-win!

Rosalie is a partner in a Canadian film production company, and works from her rented apartment all day, wrapping up in time to meet a group of friends around 4 p.m. at a local beach club. Her home is in a small city in Canada, and she finds it takes her the same time to travel to a film shoot from Mexico as it did from her home in Canada. And now that the Canadian government has implemented a two-week quarantine for all travelers from overseas, she finds it much easier to travel to filming locations from Mexico to the US, where most of her films are shot.

JP lives on his boat (really a small yacht) with his girlfriend, and he recruits talent for US law firms as an executive recruiter. He can work anywhere that he can dock and connect to Wi-Fi and uses a satellite phone back up system as well so he's free to sail away when he wants.

Freelance on Your Own Terms – From Paradise

Today, almost 40% of all jobs are done by freelancers – people who earn income reported on a 1099 form for Independent Contractors rather than on a W-2 form as company employees. And according to Forbes, this trend will continue to grow to more than half of all employees in the next few years, as employers are resisting adding to their salary and benefit burden, especially since they no longer require workers to come to the physical office.

This gives you both the time and geographic flexibility to create a portable income stream through work as an independent contractor, consultant, or freelancer.

Just about any service that you can do for an employer from an office without physically interacting with the public can be done on a contract or freelance basis.

There are a huge number of companies which offer freelance job matching in a variety of fields, though one of many different user-friendly marketplaces to buy and sell services. Some are industry-specific, others offer a wide range of service categories. You can find a list of them on my website

I have also discovered an amazing resource to learn how to excel at many different freelancing roles called Freelance University. Visit my website www.GrownUpsGuide.com for great offers on valuable training, and a very informative free webinar showing the key areas that are best for freelancers, and what skills are needed in those positions.

Freelancing is a great option, as you are generally not required to be at work at a specific time, and most positions are less than full time, providing the free time to enjoy life in paradise on your own schedule.

Explore Other Types of Businesses in Dollars

Many friends have established businesses that serve the US or Canadian customer base while delivering services here in paradise – but which are paid through a bank account in the States.

Tiffany runs an in-demand wedding planning business, coordinating gorgeous weddings at luxury beach resorts for clients whom she often meets in person for the first time when they arrive for a pre-honeymoon planning trip – or sometimes the week of the wedding itself.

Several of my friends manage rental properties owned by expats, with their monthly management fee paid in dollars into their US bank account.

Alex has a golf-cart rental business, where he delivers a golf cart to your hotel upon arrival. All rentals are prepaid in dollars into his US bank account, and he pays the local cart companies in pesos, taking a margin, and also taking advantage of a great exchange rate.

Helena provides pet sitting services in her home or in the home of clients and has been freed from the day-to-day grind of showing up for work in a store to follow her passion for caring for dogs and cats every day.

Think about your skill set, and what services you can offer that can be paid into your US bank account with PayPal, Venmo, Zelle, or Stripe.

Create Multiple Streams of Income

As a career coach in the new post-Pandemic world, I recommend to all my clients that they develop multiple streams of income.

One way to achieve that is to set up your own consulting business in your name, as a sole proprietor. Once you start generating substantial income, you may consider incorporating or converting to an LLC, but for now, setting up a small company using your name in the title allows you to build your brand, offer consulting or coaching services, or provide a range of other products and services, in a tax advantaged manner. I've prepared a free downloadable eBook available at www.LaunchYourPlanB.com. Check it out to explore options to earn money through self-employment which may allow you to move overseas fast.

There are many additional ways to support yourself in paradise, from direct sales of desired US products to online marketing, affiliate marketing, owning a bike rental shop, setting up a private service for expats like house sitting, pet sitting and babysitting, providing entertainment services, advertising and graphic design services, and much more. The goal should be to earn dollars from US customers, while living in paradise.

There are dozens of different types of employment you can explore when living in paradise, which few people think about. The ability to earn well while living overseas is so important and opens up the possibility of moving overseas earlier than you ever imagined possible, that I am in the process of writing another book about the topic, **Live and Work In Paradise: Earn Dollars. Work on Your Schedule. Live in Paradise.** You can also explore many different employment opportunities at my website www.GrownUpsGuide.com.

Benefit from Home Office Expenses or Tax Free Foreign Earned Income

Once you get settled in paradise, you may benefit from a loophole in the US Tax Code – the ability to deduct up to $100,000 of foreign earned income from your US income taxes. Learn more about this exciting option at the IRS or my website.

Alternatively, by owning your own business, or by working from a home office, even remotely, you can generally deduct a substantial part of your income by claiming home office expenses from your US income taxes. Learn more and discuss specific with your tax accountant or attorney (since I am neither). And since the tax laws change annually, you should research the latest rules and regulations directly from the IRS at www.IRS.gov.

Either way, a substantial part of your income can be earned tax free, further reducing your income requirements to support yourself in paradise.

11. START IMPLEMENTING YOUR FINANCIAL PLAN NOW

Earning additional income in paradise is just one side of the coin. The other key item is to reduce your expenses to your runaway level now. When the income and expenses balance each other, you can then run away from home worry free.

Just think — if you can eliminate expenses one-by-one to reach your runaway level budget, which you might fund through Social Security, a pension, annuity, passive investments, freelancing, multilevel sales or part-time gigs, you can runaway now!

Once you begin this journey, you will find many resources to provide valuable insights and guidance. I suggest starting with *The 4-Hour Workweek* by Tim Ferris and *The Millionaire Next Door* by Thomas J. Stanley. And don't forget *Rich Dad, Poor Dad* - another must-read guide with perspectives on how to invest your time, efforts and assets. They each provide valuable help with how to scale down, live more frugally, invest more wisely, convert liabilities into assets, generate passive income, and much more.

Become Frugal at Fifty...Or Before

To prepare to run away from home, you should be evaluating your finances and lifestyle long before you plan to move and taking important steps now to help you gain freedom much faster than you ever imagined.

The easiest and simplest way to free up cash and save more – is to spend less! Here are some basics to consider today:

Eliminate Debt

Make a concerted effort to pay off all credit cards so you can live debt free. If you have high-interest rate credit cards charged to the maximum, you will probably be paying around 24% interest. A $25,000 debt will incur interest of $500 per month, plus another $100 or $200 of principal, which is as much as many people earn in Social Security each month. A catastrophic illness or devastating job loss could rack up credit card debts like this in a relatively short time.

Some credit cards will offer you free transfers with a new high-limit card and 0% interest for the first year. You may be able to move highest-interest balances to the new cards, paying the minimum due, and paying off other high interest cards first.

Today, many credit cards are offering special concessions for people affected by the Corona virus. Call each card to see if they can reduce your interest rate. Carefully manage debt and interest rates on cards to save money, which you can then use to pay off debts.

Many unemployed or fixed-income baby boomers are too far in debt to be able to pay off such a staggering debt within a reasonable period of time. In this case, you may want to consider debt counseling, consolidation, or settlement. Search for a non-profit organization online in your area, possibly affiliated with your city, county or state government's consumer services. Your local United Way organization might also refer you to a reputable non-profit credit counseling service that can help you navigate the various options.

As a last resort, you might consider bankruptcy. Fixed income seniors with high debts can often weather a bankruptcy easier than younger individuals, since generally your primary home, modest car, IRAs and 401Ks, Social Security, Veterans benefits, and pensions are exempt from consideration or judgment. The laws are constantly changing, and I'm definitely neither an attorney nor a CPA, so you should get guidance from the appropriate professionals to help you make these difficult and painful decisions.

A great resource to explore is Upsolve.com, a non-profit organization that will empower you to file your own bankruptcy paperwork pro se, without an attorney. Check it out if you are exploring this option.

If you consult with a bankruptcy attorney, he will almost certainly recommend bankruptcy as the solution, which may or may not be your best option. This is a very important decision, so make sure you do a great deal of research and consult with several different non-profit credit counselors before taking any action.

Change Your Housing to Become Flexible, Mobile and Agile

If you are hoping to run away from home at some time in the future, you need to lay the groundwork now. Your goal should be to become more agile and ready to take advantage of opportunities to reinvent your life and move to paradise as early as possible.

You can gain a lot of flexibility by downsizing or selling your home now, so you won't be tied up with real estate issues when you are ready to move to paradise

Most of us work to pay the mortgage and property taxes each month, and traditionally one-third of all your expenses are related to housing, and another third are for food and living expenses. When you move to paradise, you should be able to cut those expenses at least in half, meaning you can earn far less to support a comfortable lifestyle. And when you realize that almost half of everything you earn in the US is spent on taxes of one kind or another, reducing expenses now can pay off quickly.

There are multiple housing options to consider. One may be right for you:

Sell Your Large Family Home and Move into a Smaller Dwelling

If your kids are gone, it makes no sense to maintain that big family home. Consider selling your large house and buying a townhouse or smaller house. When you own real estate, you are not in control of your destiny, as markets may change, and you may find yourself with a house on the market that doesn't sell for months. Right now, it's a sellers real estate market, and many houses are moving fast. But I have had two real estate sale disasters, so I am cautious about being tied down with a home to maintain when you want to be somewhere else. I also know of many people who lost their homes in prior market crashes, so cashing out and putting your nest egg in a secure financial instrument which generates cash may be the right thing to do as you prepare to run away to a new life in paradise. You can downsize now, sell your home and put money into the bank, and buy or rent a much more modest home where you can live part of the year if you choose the snowbird lifestyle.

Move Into A Leased Apartment Or House

Downsizing into a rented or leased home will free up all the equity in your home to invest in building residual income streams, and will give you a fixed lease renewal date, so you can plan months in advance with certainty about costs and timing. Most leases offer month to month renewal options, at a higher monthly rate, or early lease termination penalties, but they may be more affordable than staying behind when the time is right to move. If you go this route, discuss your plans to move out of the market with the landlord, so you can negotiate some flexibility in the lease termination terms.

Share A Home With Family Members

Knowing you plan to leave, you may make a creative arrangement with family members or long tme friends to pay them a small monthly subsidy to be able to have a furnished room in their home, preserving those treasures you absolutely can't let go at this point in your life. You can stay there until you move to paradise, and then have a place to return for occasional visits or live in during the months you find your paradise too hot or humid. Knowing you have a place to stay "back home" provides a sense of security that makes the decision to run away from home much less scary. Your room can serve as a guest room for their infrequent visitors, so it's not lost space in their home, and you know your belongings will be safe. The one key risk is that if they decide to move, you might then need to return from paradise to pack and move your belongings yourself. I just did that, and it was one of the worst weeks of my life – and expensive too.

Remember - Downsizing Takes Time and Money

Selling a house can be a very time-consuming process. It can require hundreds of hours of sorting, de-cluttering, clearing out, packing up and getting ready to move. Then it takes even more time, effort and money to fix up your house to sell it for top dollar. When someone buys a home today, their hire an inspector, who details every tiny item he can find, and the buyers may provide you with a ridiculous list of improvements or marginally necessary repairs before they will close the deal. This can delay a move for months and cost you tens of thousands of dollars.

So start the process today, so you are flexible and mobile and ready to move fast when the time is right.

And start planning your wonderful new life in paradise, as we will discuss next.

12. DESIGN YOUR FUTURE LIFESTYLE NOW

———

You are almost ready to embark on your life-transforming move to paradise. You've tried it on for size on your Beta Test, you've run all the numbers to know it is financially feasible, and you've explored opportunities to augment your income. You've taken steps to simplify your life now, free up cash, slash expenses, and lighten up the burdens of your current life.

Now you need to determine HOW you will choose to live in paradise. It's your relocation strategy – how you will get from where you are today to where you want to be in the future. You may up and move at the drop of a hat, or you may develop a five-year plan with multiple milestones along the way.

The key point is that YOU get to choose how to implement your move to paradise. And you don't have to wait until you finally reach retirement age. Regardless of your age, financial situation, or family responsibilities, you can start the transition now, by thinking creatively and finding a paradise strategy that meets your needs today.

Go Half In …or All In?

As the first step in your escape plan, you must determine how long you plan to live in paradise each year. That will determine everything else that follows and sets the stage for a series of activities to move you along your way.

I decided that a total move to my dream life was right for me and made the leap to escape to paradise full time. I gave away or sold the vast majority of my belongings, stored some others, and brought with me the bare necessities to start a brand-new life in paradise. That was my choice.

Many of my friends have decided that they will spend between six and eight months in paradise during the fall and winter and go back to be with family members and loved ones during the pleasant summer months "up north" when it's temperate there and hot and steamy here. They maintain homes in both places, and transition seamlessly and joyfully, looking forward to each transition and catching up with friends and family on each move.

Others just spend three to four months in paradise each winter, with a seasonal rental for the interim, often moving to different rentals over the years to explore and experience different areas, restaurants and local activities. They are true snowbirds, and really enjoy the lifestyle.

I've met island-lovers who come for several weeks on vacation, from two to six times a year, staying at hotels or vacation rentals, and wishing they could live this joy-filled life year-round rather than stealing away on vacation every chance they get. They feel they can't make the move full time yet because of jobs, pension requirements, businesses, kids in school, and other family responsibilities which prevent them from making the leap they so look forward to.

And many others approach their life in paradise as a blend of the above, with a splash of creativity thrown in.

There's no one best solution. There's just your solution, what feels right for you, at this point in your life. And it may change over time.

As I've explored the many different ways to live your dream, I've also learned of some alternative scenarios that are innovating and exciting and can make paradise much easier to reach and faster to attain than you ever thought possible.

Let me walk you through several lifestyle opportunities you may never have imagined before.

Let's start thinking out of the box together.

Live in Paradise Full Time

We've gone over the budget and immigration issues for full time residents already, and this is pretty simple to do. Find a great low-cost year-round rental with a nice helpful landlord and embrace life in paradise every day. Over time, you might decide to purchase your home in your new location as a great investment. You will want to get your permanent or temporary residency permit before heading to paradise, or plan to travel back on vacation or for medical checkups every six months to renew your tourist visa. When you do head back home for a visit, you can stay with family or friends, or choose a short time vacation rental or book a room on Airbnb wherever you want to hang out for a week or two. Plus, with this scenario, you can expect to have lots of family and friends come and visit you in paradise during the in-demand tourist season or when the kids and grandkids are on school vacation.

Become a Snowbird with a Home in Both Worlds

Many retirees love the snowbird lifestyle and split the year between homes in both countries. My friends Maggie and Tom, for example, have a lovely home they built here more than 15 years ago, and spend from November to April on the island each year. In April, they head back to Michigan where Maggie plants her spring garden, and they love having the grand kids spend lots of time over the summer holidays. They have no problem funding both homes with generous pensions, and find it the best of both worlds, and they love each transition. They have worked out the bugs of finding reliable help to maintain both homes during their absence and come home to a house that is clean and well maintained and ready to pick up where they left off half a year before.

Rent Full Time to Vacation Part Time

For many people, this is a life-changing option they just never realized was possible.

Debi has a family farm she inherited in Washington state, and has responsibilities that keep her tied to the States part of the year. Her solution: she has rented a cute one-bedroom apartment and rotates between the two homes every month or so. Her island life costs her a flat $500 a month which is easily funded by her own Social Security pension and her widow's benefits. She leaves her clothes in the closet and food in the fridge, tossing out or freezing perishables as she walks out the door for a month. A quick trip to the grocery store and she's back up and enjoying life in paradise in just a few hours after the plane lands.

Many of my friends have similarly flexible lifestyles and maintain their pied-a-terre in the island year-round for what you would pay for a two-week vacation at a hotel.

Create a Family and Friends Time Share

I was recently hanging out in the pool at a beach club and met three best friends who are all airline employees who are able to fly for free. They yearned for the tropical lifestyle, had flexible work schedules, could get here for free – but didn't realize how inexpensively you could live in paradise. I told them about the option to rent monthly for what you would pay for a couple of nights in a North Beach hotel and encouraged them to set up a family and friends time share.

The idea is to rent a two-bedroom home, like mine, which would cost them less than $1,000 a month with weekly cleaning service and all utilities, and split the cost between four different families, at just $250 a month each family. They can choose their bedroom of preference and leave their clothes in the closet and their toothbrush in the sink or tuck them into an owner's closet for privacy if desired. Each family would have the right to 26 weeks of bedroom rental of one bedroom (half a year!), or 13 weeks rental of both bedrooms. They can divvy up their 26 weeks however they agree, staying in one room, or taking over the full apartment with both bedrooms for a family get together. If they want to go all in, they could buy an older car or golf cart, so they can also enjoy easy reliable transportation. The secret to this will be to make sure the landlord understands the plan to share among family, as landlords will generally not approve of subletting the apartment or offering it for a vacation rental. And it's also critical to share your runaway home only with others you know and like and have the same approach to living as you do. This is an incredibly easy and simple plan, and can be lifechanging, so I'm amazed that everyone isn't doing it.

Other Creative Lifestyle Options

I've met many people who live in paradise on unique schedules driven by work obligations, but which can serve as inspiration to guide you to an innovative and happy solution.

I met Barbara, who has been the Practice Manager for a chain of 7 orthodontic clinics in Southern California. She and her husband bought land on the island, and over several years built a charming beach home., vacationing frequently throughout the process. When it was finished, she gave notice to the owner of the clinics that she was going to retire and move permanently to Mexico. Her boss and long-term friend simply refused to accept the resignation, begging her to stay, and offering her any kind of concession she wanted. As a result, she now works from the first to the tenth of every month in the office, staying at her daughter's house nearby during those ten days. On the 11th, she flies back to Mexico, where she forgets about work until she has to head back stateside on the last day of the month. Everyone knows that she can only be reached during that 10-day window, and she works long days to squeeze in all the obligations of her important job. Since she knows exactly what dates she will be in the States, she can book her non-stop airline ticket months in advance and gets great deals for as little as $350 round trip. She continues to earn top dollar, spends time with her daughter and grandchildren each month, and still can schedule three weeks a month in paradise.

I met another woman, Esther, who is a hair stylist in a tony Beverly Hills salon, where the rent on her chair and station is over $3,000 a month. She has partnered with a friend and coworker, Marie, to share both the workstation and the island apartment in two-week increments. They each book their respective clients when they are scheduled to be at the salon, and both make almost the same income working half time that they did working full time and paying astronomical southern California rents.

Carole is a psychiatrist who specializes in the evaluation and medication management of rehab, nursing home and hospice patients in San Antonio, Texas. Three year ago, while on vacation in Cancun, she stumbled across a charming bungalow for the incredibly low price of $67,000 and made an offer on the spot. She has invested another $15,000 in upgrades, but still owns her dream retirement home for what some people pay for a new car. She is not ready for retirement, so she schedules her work to be heavy at the beginning of the month, allowing her to take the last 10 days of each month to fly to Cancun to enjoy her home in the tropics. She spends her days snorkeling the reefs of Isla Mujeres, soaking in the rays on the white sandy beaches, exploring Mayan ruins and swimming in spring-fed cenotes, adding lovely finishing touches to her home in the tropics, and dining out with friends. She is a naturalized US citizen, speaks fluent Spanish, and is a fan of live theater. She has an annual membership to two different performing arts centers where she attends at least one or two live performances during every trip for what she would pay for movie tickets in the States.

Maria and Don have a different approach. Maria retired from her high-powered job in software sales and decided to follow her dream of opening her own Italian fine dining restaurant on the water's edge with breathtaking views. Her husband Dan owned and operated a commercial construction company in New England, and they designed and built a beautiful restaurant with their comfortable owner's suite in the back. Maria runs the day-to-day activities of the restaurant, preparing fresh pasta and home-made mozzarella daily, and creating amazing delicacies she learned from her Italian mother and grandmother. Dan is the social one in the family, and happily greets guests and provides wine samples to help diners' select the perfect wine to accompany the meal. Once a month, he flew back to New England for a week to keep his finger in the construction business and stays with his kids when back in the States. Dan's profitable business funded the construction of their home and restaurant in paradise and provided ongoing cash flow to take the pressure off Maria, especially during the difficult Covid shut down when many restaurants were forced out of business. He recently sold the business and now stays year around in paradise, greeting friends who visit the lovely restaurant year after year as tourists, or frequently if they live here like I do.

Some people enjoy life in paradise on a boat or a small yacht. I met Mike and Patrick through mutual friends and learned that the two brothers bought their dream 45-foot sailboat on a whim to run away from home and sail around the Caribbean. The boat has been anchored at a local marina while they do what seems like never-ending repairs, and the brothers are enjoying island life. Patrick was a high-powered tech expert, but is recovering from a serious illness and currently on disability. Mike is an amazing brother and sidekick, so he quit his job as a datamining expert to join Patrick on their sailing adventure of a lifetime. To bring in extra income, and to keep up with his profession and remain marketable, Mike works small freelance projects for a former employer and a couple of small clients, with consulting fees deposited in his US bank account.

Likewise, my chiropractor, Dr. Ben, lives on a boat at a popular local marina. He's selling his home in another part of the Yucatan and negotiating the purchase of a 44-foot Catamaran. In the interim, he's boat sitting at the marina, and performing minor maintenance repairs in lieu of rent. In exchange for free chiropractic care for his family, the marina owner allows him to use an elevated open-air deck nestled into the branches of a huge Banyan tree overlooking the marina as an open-air office for chiropractic treatments. It feels like I am having a back adjustment in the tree house of the Swiss Family Robinson!

I've met dozens of people who live on boats large or small, and they love the mobile yet very social lifestyle that boat-living brings. It's an option that wouldn't be right for me, but might be right for you. And remember, it's not forever, just for right now.

Which Lifestyle Option Do You Choose?

Once you explore the creative options available, you are empowered to choose how you will venture into your new life overseas. There is no one best way. The challenge is to find what works best for you today, and then start down your path to freedom.

You may well feel that you can't walk away from a pension that vests in a couple of years, or need to wait until the last child leaves for college, or you are able to finally get Social Security and Medicare before you can give up a job which pays for those important medical insurance benefits. Those are important considerations which guide your choices.

At the same time, one of these lifestyle scenarios may be the bridge to your life of joy, now or in the future. You don't have to wait to retire to live in paradise. You can start on the journey now, with creative lifestyle options that are affordable today, even on a modest budget.

Once you have made the choice of how you will get to paradise, you are ready for the next step – creating and executing your step-by-step plan.

13. CREATE YOUR STEP-BY-STEP PLAN TO LEAVE

————

Your lifestyle vision will determine what you do with your home, belongings, finances, pets and much more.

Once you have a clear picture of what your life in Paradise will look like, you can start to create a detailed plan to achieve it.

There are just 3 major decisions to make based on your lifestyle choice, and they are the steps you need to make "back home" to free yourself to make your move to paradise.

Let's get started.

Who Will Go with You?

Of course, you will be going to your new life, but what about other people in your life? Will you be going solo, like I did, or with a partner? Or maybe the whole family - spouse and kids? Or perhaps you will be bringing a special needs adult child, like Sheila, who finds it possible to hire quality round the clock caregivers in paradise – even though negotiating potholed streets and uneven sidewalks with a wheelchair is tricky.

It's important that you involve each of your loved ones in the decision-making process, so that everyone supports your choices, and they have their needs met at the same time.

That also means speaking with extended family members who are no longer living with you – grown children, siblings concerned for your safety, best friends and mentors, etc.

If not, they can be negative voices sapping your energy and eroding your confidence when something doesn't go quite as planned.

There are lots of options, and I want to share some experiences others have had to help you address this issue.

Going Solo

Moving to paradise alone is perhaps the easiest decision to make, but often the scariest one to execute. While you only have to accommodate your own needs, you may face loneliness, doubts, fears, and concerns about security, especially if you are a single woman like myself.

A good strategy is to make sure you engage with many people during your Beta Test and the weeks and months leading up to your trip to ensure you have someone who will greet you, make you feel welcome, and help you navigate the many challenges you face.

I was lucky to connect with my friend Helena, a French woman who visited Isla 32 years ago, fell in love with the Island, and has lived here ever since. She met me the day I arrived for good and hosted me to a lovely lunch to welcome me to my new life.

My move was made much easier by the visit of my cousin Sara to celebrate her 50th birthday just four days after I moved to paradise, giving me lots of opportunities to go out, meet people, discover new restaurants and beach clubs, and explore my new home. By the time she left ten days later, I was well established, had met lots of new friends, and was confident in my new life. Having a friend and supporter join you temporarily as you embark on your journey will make it so much more fun and less scary.

Going As A Couple

Moving to paradise as a twosome is much less scary, and easier if your visions for the future are aligned. You are two individuals whose own needs must be met, so while you will often be doing things as a couple, make sure you each have solo time to expand your network and explore on your own. Let him go to the local sports bar to watch the playoffs, while you play mah jongg or Rummy Cube with your woman's group, for example. You may want to engage in salsa lessons as a couple, but then he may want to join a CrossFit gym while you join a local yoga group. Volunteering for a nonprofit organization helps you each find a meaningful role in your new home. He might want to sit vigil for sea turtles as they nest overnight, and you might want to volunteer at a special needs school. And of course, there are many joint activities that you can do as a couple that you will both enjoy.

Moving With Minor Children

I know many couples who moved with their children, which brings the unique challenges of finding schooling, babysitters or nannies, helping the kids make friends, and securing transportation. When Jeff and Rhett moved to this tiny island with their five-year-old daughter, they did not find the schooling they wanted, and for the first six months home schooled her. Soon they met other families with similar challenges, and they formed a community Montessori-type school where between six and ten families educate their children in the equivalent of a two-room schoolhouse. They contract a US teacher for the year, who uses the opportunity to live in paradise on her own, and a local Spanish-speaking teacher at a much lower costs, which ensures the kids learn Spanish in addition to their lessons in English.

Home schooling has evolved today to be easy, affordable, and logistically very feasible, and even more so since the pandemic has forced so many children into home schooling. You might not even need to change the school for your children, as many schools are offering year-round remote learning by video conferencing. See what you can negotiate with the school administrators – you may be amazed by their flexibility.

Another option is to leave the kids behind for their final year of high school to live with a friends or family members, rather than disrupting their graduation plans and tearing them away from their friends. And then you can host the kids to your life in paradise for all the school holidays – it may be a win for everyone. They may even be much sought after if they can bring a best friend back for a summer vacation trip!

Moving with younger children is probably easiest, as quality childcare is incredibly inexpensive – and they will grow up learning the local language as native speakers – a great benefit!

Peter and Analise waited until both their sons were in college to make their final move. They had established a well patronized restaurant here in Mexico and worked full time in the tropics during the busy winter tourist season for more than 10 years, and returned to their famed seaside restaurant at their inn in New England during the summer, taking advantage of both peak earning periods. Just last year they sold their State-side home and the inn in Maine, and moved their residency in Austin, Texas, a low tax state, by buying a condo near several different colleges. Both boys live together, and there's a room for mom and dad to stay when they visit several times a year. And of course, the boys look forward to school holidays and lazy summers in their parents' paradise home, equipped with an ocean view and a small motorboat for water activities.

Moving With Special Needs Children

Sheila is a 60+ year old widow who has spent most of her adult lifetime caring for her handicapped daughter with severe Downs Syndrome. She was trapped in her own home, carrying for her adult special needs child who required full time supervision. With caregiving rates in the $15 - $20 per hour range in the States, she was trapped without a way out while living in her home in Alabama. But by moving to paradise, she was able to hire a full-time live-in caregiver for just $100 per week – what she would spend back home for an afternoon off to go to the doctor or to have a rare lunch out with a friend. And with the extended network of neighbors and her caregiver's family, she has multiple backup resources in a community where everyone chips in to care for needy children as a whole, grateful for a couple of dollars of tips for additional care.

She had to look hard to find the perfect ground-floor handicap-accessible rental home, with a bright sunny patio in the back yard so her daughter can sit outside with minimal supervision. But she was able to find a lovely two-bedroom house for just $650 per month, allowing them to live like royalty compared to their limited existence back home.

Navigating the streets and sidewalks with a wheelchair is a challenge, but they manage, and with the help of the local caregiver, they can get the wheelchair loaded onto the back of a golf cart to explore when the spirit moves them.

Parents and Adult Children

Karen moved to paradise more than five years ago, while in her early 60s, after losing her husband in the States. Her only daughter Melissa visited her frequently from her home in Texas, due to business dealings in Mexico City. A telecommunication professional, Melissa identified the need for high- speed internet services for expat residents, and founded a local internet company that offers a package of unique services in English to support the expatriate community. She eventually moved here where she can spend quality time with her mom while also pursuing her entrepreneurial business. Mom and daughter each have their own homes for independence and their own network of friends, but they often are seen together at social events, and enjoy the rooftop happy hour on Wednesdays at a favorite upscale restaurant overlooking the Caribbean shoreline.

On the other hand, Tiffany has lived in Isla for the past 15 years, and has developed a vibrant wedding planning business, and has established herself as one of the best wedding planners in the country. She shares her rented home with boyfriend Gonzalo and three dogs. Tiffany's mom Sandy was recently widowed and has decided to move to Isla to be near her daughter. She already has a network of friends her age from prior visits and has recently rented a comfortable two-bedroom home with an ocean view for just $500 per month – a fraction of what it would cost to live back in Minnesota.

Moving with Aged Parents

My friend, Carola, was supporting her 87-year-old widowed father in an assisted living facility in San Diego, with the total cost of care in excess of $6,000 every month. His Social Security and Medicare benefits contributed about $2,200 to his care, and family members were left on the hook for the balance of $3,800 each month. He was unhappy with the care he received, as he did not want to be "institutionalized", but the family had no other way to provide care for him after Carola let the area due to a job change.

When Carola decided to move back to live in Mexico City, she convinced her dad to move with her to a nearby independent care facility in Puebla, about an hour's drive from her house. At first, he was hesitant, but after just a week, he loved it. The facility was gorgeous, with a spectacular outdoor pool, gym, beautiful grounds, a choice of restaurant-like dining facilities, and the care was spectacular – all for just $1,000 per month. He met many other people he enjoys spending time with and is actually dating another resident. He has access to private transportation, can go out for meals, movies, and entertainment, and enjoys round the clock care which he can direct, rather than being told what to do by staff nurses. His Social Security pays the full cost of the home and leaves him with lots of money to enjoy the local restaurant and entertainment scene. His two sons try to visit at least once a year from their homes in New York and France, and Carola takes a bus to visit him for the weekend once a month. Because of the inexpensive labor costs in Mexico, he can live in the equivalent of an upscale apartment complex, while receiving excellent on-demand care and services.

In retrospect, if I had realized I could have moved to paradise five years ago, I could have opted to care for my mom here in the same way. I now have the network of friends and supporters who could have supported me in the challenging role of caregiver, for much less than I paid to have her live in a nursing home or private care home in Texas. Unfortunately, by the time I realized that I could live the life of my dreams while comfortably taking care of my mom with dementia, she was too weak and disoriented to make the trip. But it is a valid option for others to explore as you wrestle with the unpleasant options of caring for loved ones in their declining years while facing exorbitant costs for care in the US.

Choosing End of Life Care in Paradise

I know of several people in the local international community who have lost loved ones due to chronic terminal diseases, and after much discussion and soul searching, they jointly opted to live out their last days in paradise, paying for their care at local prices, rather than return to be institutionalized "back home".

Lydia's husband, Lance died after a long battle with Lou Gehrig's disease. As Canadians, they could have opted to go back to Canada to have him hospitalized there, or return to live in Canada and try to care for him at home using hospice support. After extensive testing and medical consultation concerning the relentless progress of the disease, they felt that they could not make any medical interventions to extend the quality of life or reverse the ravage of the disease. They opted to stay in their lovely island home, where they had a large network of friends and local caregivers, including the local doctor who made frequent home visits. They found it was very affordable to have almost 24-hour care in Mexico, with a male driver who could pick Lawry up and move him from bed to wheelchair, and bathe him, for less than $20 per day. He died peacefully in the home he loved, looking out at the ocean waves breaking on the Caribbean shore. It was a choice they both made, given the irreversible nature of the disease, and in retrospect, Lynda is very happy they made the choices they did.

Similarly, Laura her husband John had lived on the Island for more than four years, when John's battle with cancer took a turn for the worse. They too chose to remain in their home in paradise and enjoy the beautiful warm weather and breathtaking ocean views as John's health continued to decline day by day. Laura loves to bake, and her hobby is baking cakes and delicious deserts, and John kept her company in the kitchen from the comfort of his wheelchair. She swam every day in their private pool, finding respite from the arduous burden of around-the-clock caregiving, and on good days, their burly driver Noel would lift John into the pool for a respite from being wheelchair-bound. Doctors and nurses made frequent house calls, and they had help in the house throughout the day, and support was a five-minute phone call away if any emergencies arose overnight. When John finally passed, his body was transported to Cancun by ambulance, where he was cremated for just $700 – compared to the many thousands one would pay for a funeral or cremation in the States. His ashes are scattered on the beach in front of their oceanside home, and Laura talks to him each morning when she sits on the patio enjoying her coffee and watching the beautiful sunrise.

The passing of a loved one is always terribly sad, and family members and caregivers are unfortunately forced to make the best choice from among many unpleasant alternatives. For a number of people, choosing to live out the final days of their life in paradise is the best choice for them, and it's an option to explore if you find yourself facing such painful decisions as well.

Ensuring a Successful Move To Paradise

There are many different options for living in paradise and moving with family members is a great option. There are, however, some considerations to ensure success. The key is for all family members to be open to change, and flexible in their needs. If you have one family member who is adamantly against the move, then he probably should not be forced to join you, as it will make everyone in the family miserable. Alternative living conditions may be needed to accommodate that family member.

Likewise, anyone who is negative, a naysayer or a constant complainer will find way too many things to complain about and can cast a negative pall over all the family members, spoiling the adventure for everyone. Remember, happiness begins inside, and if you are not happy with yourself where you are today, you probably won't be happier with yourself when you move to another location without fixing your personal self-image.

Years ago, I knew a family which was being transferred to Brazil for my husband's company. The 12-year-old son was an extremely demanding and picky eater and refused to eat anything except peanut butter. He was inflexible and critical of everything and didn't want to move and leave his friends behind. We knew right away that the move would be a disaster. It ended up practically tearing the family apart, as the mom and son ended up moving back to the States, leaving the dad and older son to fend for themselves in Brazil. Within a year, they all moved back home, and the experience negatively affected the dad's career with the company, all driven by the inflexible attitude of one family member forced to make a move he did not want.

To be a successful candidate for a move to paradise, you want everyone to be positive, upbeat, and open to change and adventure. The willingness to learn a new language is important, and good candidates for a relocation to paradise should be open to different races, ethnicities and cultures. And you want to make sure that anyone who is going to preface every sentence with "Back home we do it this way…" stays back home.

What Do I Do with The House?

We've previously discussed housing options, and the potential to start the downsizing option well in advance of your move. And we've discussed creative ways to structure living arrangements in the US to reduce costs and provide more flexibility.

Now it's time to put your housing choices into action.

If You Are Renting

If you are currently renting your house, make sure you know the lease terms – date of contract renewal, lease cancellation notification requirements, return of deposits, inspection process, stayover clauses, and the like. Can you terminate the lease early, or must you wait to the end of the lease term? If you want to extend month-to-month until you are ready to move, what will the costs be? Many leases require a 60-day notice period and will require you to show the house to potential tenants during the notice period. Often landlords have exorbitant stay-over costs to encourage tenants to move out on time, and you want to be aware of them in advance to avoid unpleasantness. You should also be proactively communicating with your landlord, letting him know of your plans to make a major life change, to be able to ask for special accommodations if needed. When I finally moved from my leased house, the property manager was very accommodating, did the walk through in the morning and actually cut the deposit refund check that very afternoon so I could deposit it in the bank before leaving for the airport the next day.

Moving from Your Own Home

What you do with a home you own is predicated by the choice of your future lifestyle. Are you moving full time, going as a snowbird for the winter, or just vacationing whenever possible?

Simply Keep Your Home

If you plan to move to paradise part time and are able and want to keep your US or Canadian home, your move choices are so much easier. You can choose to downsize over time to meet your new lifestyle needs, or just continue in the family home you've lived in for years. Key will be to find reliable maintenance help to keep the home in tip top shape and ready when you head back home for the summer.

This might also be the easiest way to ease into life overseas, and I know many people who have rented or bought island homes and transitioned between them every year. Many start out living in their dream locations just a few months a year, and then choosing to stay longer and longer each year.

For example, Maggie and her husband Tom fully embrace their island lifestyle and are actively engaged in many programs to support the people of the island that they love. They have founded a wonderful scholarship program which pays for local high school graduates to go to a Mexican university, and more than 25 local students have received university degrees which would have been impossible to attain without the scholarship program. They also set up and ran a free English language school for more than 10 years to help local children gain the skills they will need to thrive in a tourism economy.

At the same time, they also love their home in Wisconsin, and head back to the States around Easter each year, returning in the fall after spending Thanksgiving with their kids and grandkids. Maggie takes special joy in planting and tending a summer garden of flowers, herbs and vegetables, which they eat all summer long. And they relish their return each fall, to dive back into the expatriate life in paradise. They live in a lovely ocean front ranch house they built more than 12 years ago, with a big front patio with a 180-degree view of the ocean, and a big grassy fenced-in yard along the ocean front road. They own a small two-story house in the busy residential area of the island which they rent to expats on a long-term basis, and have reliable help cultivated over the many years they have lived on the island who take care of anything that arises when they are gone. Tom is a retired firefighter, and Maggie retired from her job as a physical therapist, and their generous pensions allow them to comfortably maintain homes in both worlds.

They have learned to effectively handle the opening and closing of each home annually, and are old hands at forwarding mail, winterizing the car which will be stored in the garage, and sealing up the Wisconsin home for a long winter.

Downsize To A Smaller Home

Another option for people who want to have homes in each market is to downsize to a smaller, less expensive home first, so you can afford to maintain two homes for the cost of just one larger home in the US. This might mean a move to a smaller condominium, townhouse, or apartment, alleviating the need to worry about yard care and maintaining the sidewalks free of snow in the cold winter.

If that meets your need for an initial transition, then the proceeds from the house sale can fund the smaller home or condo, as well as your home in paradise, and the rest of the funds can plump up your cash reserves or investment accounts, boosting your financial security. This process can take many months or even years, as you sell one home and move into another, and can be stressful at the time. However, it can provide you with your home base in the States, while reducing your cash flow needs to become a good investment over time.

Keep And Share Your Home

Another option is to keep your home and share it with others. You may have a relative or friend move in with you, or you may invite one of your grown kids to live in your home as they're just starting out. They may be expected to pay the utilities and provide the maintenance help that you will need, although you might be well advised to pay for periodic cleaning, maintenance, yard and pool care, and the like to avoid unpleasant surprises until you are absolutely certain that they will maintain your home the way you expect.

Since you will be gone for significant periods of time, this will allow your family members to enjoy their own privacy, and yet welcome you for the short periods when you come back.

A challenge may arise if their lifestyle changes and they no longer want or are able to live in your home – a job change, relocation, the need to care for other family members, or the opportunity to buy their own home. That would necessitate a return trip, and making other arrangements to occupy the home, or decide to keep it unoccupied while you are overseas, which means you will be paying the full cost of maintaining the home.

When you allow someone else to live in your home during your absence, there is a certain risk involved, and you need to have a clear-cut contract or written agreement which specifies the details of the arrangement.

You also must be careful to protect your legal rights as a homeowner, and make sure you know your rights as a landlord, to avoid the unpleasant situation of having to evict a tenant or squatter if things don't work out as planned. From time to time, you will hear news stories of parents suing to evict their grown son from the basement. It is bizarre – but it does happen.

The point is, you can decide to share your home with others to reduce your expenses, and then take the savings you have and invest in your living expenses in paradise.

Share The US Home Of A Friend Or Family Member

The flip side of that scenario is to move out of your home, either selling or renting it, and move in with a friend or family member, to limit your monthly expenses and maintenance responsibilities. It also provides them with a source of additional income, in exchange for providing a space to store your treasures.

That's what I chose to do. I and gave away or sold 95% of my belongings through progressive moves and downsizings but ended up with a nucleus of treasures I was not ready to part with. I didn't have a family member who could conveniently and inexpensively store them, so I agreed with a longtime friend Jackie to contribute $400 per month towards the rent of a home, where I could furnish a second bedroom with my prized belongings, and a China hutch filled with my China and cut crystal that I bought at the factory in Portugal more than 40 years ago. The bedroom looks like an art gallery, with paintings and prints hung on every available space, but I know my treasures are safe and won't get damaged in storage or affected by weather. The closet is full of clothing that's not appropriate for the tropics, I've got bookshelves with that nucleus of books and notebooks that I treasure, and I've got a trunk of family heirlooms I can't yet part with. Jackie uses my bedroom as a guest room, and as long as the bedding is freshly laundered when I arrive, I'm happy. My medical records, business records, tax files, college diplomas, and personal memoirs are tucked in a file cabinet in the closet. On the rare occasions I travel back to the States for business or medical visits, I bring back two or three suitcases packed to the brim with items I want to bring down with me, and slowly by surely my favorite belongings are making their way to my new home.

Rent Your Home for Appreciation and Cash Flow

Many people decide to keep their home and rent or lease it for long periods of time to generate cash flow, while keeping the right to move back in at some point in the future. This requires excellent support of a well-qualified person who will manage your property or hiring a professional property management firm to handle anything that arises. They will determine rental rates based on market demand, show and lease the property, provide maintenance support as needed, and deal with homeowners' associations or city rules and regulations. You should have little or no interaction with the tenants, unless there is an unexpected expense to approve. As a baseline, expect to pay a typical residential property management firm between 8 – 12% of the monthly rental value of the property, plus expenses. Some companies may charge a flat rate as low as $100 per month. Interview multiple property management firms and seek recommendations both online and from people you know, to select a firm with the experience and expertise that allows you to turn over your home and live worry-free in paradise.

Go All Out - Sell the House and Give Up Your Home Base

When you decide to move full time, you may opt to sell your current house, and no longer maintain a residence "back home." It allows you to invest all your housing assets into generating cash flow or increasing your retirement funds. You will still need to establish a US address for state residency and tax issues, as well as setting up mail delivery and handling for important communication. A good option is to rent a virtual mailbox, as we discussed in Chapter 8.

Selling your home takes time and money and can be very stressful. You will need to either move out and professionally stage your home or declutter and get rid of many of your belongings before putting the house on the market, so it shows optimally. You will also have to invest a substantial amount of money in cleaning, painting, and updating your home prior to putting it on the market. Your real estate agent may advise you of the need to modernize the home to get top dollar in sales, and you may find yourself paying thousands to replace brass fixtures with the newer contemporary metals popular today, replacing carpet with wooden flooring, or installing granite countertops like I did. You may find yourself pressure washing the driveway, repainting the home inside and out, trimming trees, and updating landscaping to help market your home.

Today, anyone who buys a home will hire a home inspector, who will go through every inch of your residence and note any major and minor item that is imperfect or out of code, and many buyers will demand that every item be fixed, replaced or repaired as part of the terms of the contract.

This whole process takes time and money and is often out of your control. If you plan to sell your home as part of your move to paradise, start early by interviewing realtors, asking their opinions about needed updates, getting competitive market estimates, requesting recommendations for pricing and asking for projected closing costs and net receipts. Make sure you ask for referrals from neighbors who have recently sold their homes. Then start making the needed repairs early on. I actually hired my own independent home inspector so I could be prepared in advance, and the new purchasers were satisfied with the report and subsequent updating so they did not require a new inspection, but you can't count on it.

You can also estimate that it will cost you around 10% of the final sales value to sell your home in closing costs, title insurance, marketing fees, and the like – in addition to the maintenance and updating costs which you will have to fund in advance of listing the house.

And make contingency plans for different sales closing dates. What if your house sells the first day it is listed, and the new buyers want to move in fast

– will you be ready to get out earlier than anticipated? And what if the sale drags on for several months, or is cancelled – like two of my home sales were? How will you handle having the house on the market months longer than anticipated? Plan for different contingencies so that your move goes smoothly despite the lack of control you exert over the process. And keep your eye on the goal – all the hassles of the house sale with last minute glitches are just part and parcel of the process of freeing yourself to move to paradise.

As hard as dealing with your house is, the next phase is even more painful and challenging!

14. WHAT DO I DO WITH MY STUFF?

────

By far, the hardest part of moving to paradise for me was dealing with the "stuff" of my life. We live in such affluence in our country that many people have so many belongings that they can become a burden rather than a blessing.

You Need Less Stuff in Paradise

One of the freeing aspects of moving to paradise is learning how little you really need.

That was one of the freeing aspects of moving to paradise. I moved into a two-bedroom furnished home and was happy bringing just three suitcases and a dog on my lap on the plane. Imagine – all I needed to live happily in a new land was 150 pounds of total belongings! So why are we burdened with owning, managing and storing so much more in our US homes?

In my process of learning to run away from home, I discovered that living with little 'stuff' is freeing and exhilarating – and it is much easier than the process of getting rid of the 'stuff.'

When you move to paradise, and if you choose to rent a furnished home, you will need limited amounts of clothing, shoes, jewelry, toiletries, communication devices like your laptop and phone, and tools you need for your remote job. It really is that simple. Over time I have acquired more stuff, but I selectively purchase new items after really thinking about them. I debated internally for several weeks to decide if I really wanted to spend $15 on a new hand mixer – after I had just sold my Kitchen Aid freestanding mixer with all the attachments for almost nothing.

You May Need Different Stuff in Paradise

One thing many people don't realize is that you need different belongings in paradise, and that difference may make your US belongings obsolete in your new life.

I live year-round dressed in about 10 or 15 lightweight sleeveless dresses, and half a dozen pair of pretty sandals and a pair of sneakers and beach shoes. I have 2 pairs of dark slacks for the few chilly days every year, and a couple of long sleeve blouses and a washable jacket or two. I do have about six swimsuits, and I switch them out for different tan lines. During the steamy days of summer, I often wear my swimsuit under my little sleeveless dress, so I can dip into the beach or pool whenever I wish. I really don't need much more to be happy and live well! And nobody else does either. Everybody is too focused on looking at the breathtaking water or blazing sunset to wonder if you've recently worn that outfit before. It just doesn't matter in a world where everyone is living a minimalist lifestyle.

When I look at my US closet, I don't have a need for the evening gowns, cocktail dresses, business suits and matching silk blouses, winter clothes, my fur stole, dozens of blouses, and all those high heels that formed part of my everyday wardrobe in the past. They just don't fit in to my new lifestyle.

Because I travel throughout Mexico and the US on occasion to teach or lecture, I do have several outfits appropriate for travel back to the big city. I actually brought back a raw silk suit and shell this last trip, and a couple of pair of low pumps, and a butter-soft unstructured suede Chicos jacket. But they are tucked in the back of my four-foot-wide closet to pull out only when I need to leave paradise to go back to the other world. And I don't have any gear for winter at all!

Most men likewise wear lightweight knit or canvas shorts, T-shirts, breathable cotton short sleeved shirts, a swimsuit or two, and a pair of sandals, sneakers, and deck shoes. When you move full time, you may want to add a pair of jeans and khaki slacks, a couple of cotton shirts, a lightweight jacket or hoodie, and perhaps leather shoes for more formal occasions. You really don't need much more than that. Toss in a couple of swim trunks, and an occasional pair of jeans, and you're done. You can generally fit all this into one large suitcase or hockey bag. Grab a knapsack for carrying towels to the beach, and you're ready to live well in paradise.

Your home furnishings are similar in many ways. The beautiful furniture, artwork, rugs, and accessories that look so great in your "up north" home probably won't fit into your pared-back lifestyle in paradise. Instead, you may want light weight or airy fabrics, light colored woods like bamboo and teak to avoid termites and wood rot. Colors are brighter and bolder, motifs are tropical rather than subdued, and sunlight streaming in your windows becomes a design feature to deal with. Floors are tile or stone, not carpeted. Walls are painted concrete block, not drywall, and it is difficult to hang artwork and mirrors. So even though you have lovely furnishings, they may not fit into your new life, and you will want to leave them behind to embrace your new lifestyle.

When you live back home, surrounded with the "stuff" of your existence, it's hard to image a life of such simplicity. You have to experience it to understand it. And it is wonderfully freeing.

At the same time, it's tough to keep feeling that same way when you face the challenge of dealing with all the physical belongings of your existence.

If you've opted to keep a home "up north", and move to paradise part time, you may not need to deal with downsizing your "stuff" right away. It's always beneficial, but not critical. You can take the summers when you are back "home" to cull down belongings, and slowly downsized and lighten up. However, if you decide to completely reinvent your life and make a major lifestyle shift, downsize, or move permanently to paradise, then you will be forced to deal with your belongings.

Categories of Belongings

In my process of moving to paradise, I discovered that it's helpful to categorize everything you own and may want to keep, not by its physical structure, but rather by your level and type of emotional attachment to it. The key categories that I have identified are:

- **Treasures that Bring Joy** – Special items that make you smile when you see them, and often evoke memories of a special occasion in your life. You definitely want to keep them – somewhere.
- **Family Legacy** – Decide who will carry on the family heritage when you no longer can
- **Legal and Personal Obligations** – There are documents you are legally obligated to own and maintain – what do you do with them?
- **Basic Necessities** – These are the items you use every day, and will carry to your new home in your suitcases
- **Everything Else** – It's amazing how much of your belongings fit in this category. And you will be shocked to learn how easy it is to replace things for a pittance when you decide that you need them again.

Seven Ways to Deal with Your Belongings

As you evaluate everything you own, ask yourself how you want to deal with it. You can't ignore its existence. Every single thing that you bring into your house has to leave again when you do. Everything you own must be dealt with one of these 7 ways:

Will you:

- **Bring it with you** - Will it fit into your suitcase? With only 50 lbs. per suitcase, is this more important than another belonging you will have to leave behind? And will it fit into your new minimalized lifestyle in paradise?
- **Ship it** - Shipping is expensive – how much is it really worth to you? Can you replace it easier than transport it? And will it fit into your new bar-boned lifestyle when it gets here?

- **Sell it** - You will be shocked and distressed at how little you will receive for your treasured possessions – even ones you paid thousands for – if you are able to sell them at all!
- **Put it in storage** – and pay a monthly fee to maintain it in limbo?
- **Give it away** - Can you gift it to someone who will value it?
- **Donate it to charity** - This is the default for anything you don't know what to do with. There is a reason there is a Goodwill Donation Station on practically every corner!
- **Throw it away** - Believe it or not, many charities won't take many of your belongings. Furniture, mattresses, electronics, food, office supplies, large appliances, and much more may be rejected as unmarketable. You may actually have to pay to have unwanted possessions disposed of.

As you make your relocation plan, ask yourself which of these seven choices you will make for each item you own. It does make it so much easier to know that long term, you can't just ignore it. When the day comes to move out of your home, and you expect the new buyers or the landlord to do a walkthrough of the property you are vacating, every single thing you own must be gone. Plan now what you will do with each and every item and start the process today, as it can be totally overwhelming if you leave it to the last minute.

What Will I Do with My Car?

You face many of the same challenges in dealing with your car as you do with your household goods. Will you keep it in storage, sell it, give it away, or bring it with you to paradise?

One option is to bring your car with you to Mexico when you move, either as a temporary or permanent resident. If you are a snowbird, traveling back and forth each year on a 180-day tourist visa, it may be a very cost-effective option, especially if you will be staying near the border.

You may decide to keep it stored back home or lend or give it to family members or friends.

Alternatively, you may choose to donate it to charity for a tax write off and to save time and hassle.

Or you may decide to do what I did – sell your car in the States and purchase a new or used vehicle when you get settled in your new home.

Whatever you choose to do, now is the time to start thinking about your cars or personal vehicles and your move to paradise plan, and how to handle each vehicle.

Take Baby Steps to Deal with Your Stuff Now

I could write a whole book on how to deal with the "stuff" of life, but I've put the highlights into my companion book – **The Runaway Roadmap – Your Step-buy-Step Guide to Escape to Paradise and Live Richly on any Budget.** It's available on Amazon and on my website www.GrownUpsGuide.com.

But don't buy it now. Wait until you are ready to start to implement your move before becoming focused on the million little details that can distract you from your vision.

For now, just embrace the reality that you can free yourself from the burden of owning and managing so much unnecessary "stuff" that it weighs you down so you can't fly to freedom. And start taking baby steps by examining your possessions and letting go all of those that don't bring you joy or fill a need in your life today. It will make your future easier, whether you decide to move to paradise or stay right where you are.

What Do I Do with My Pets?

The great new is that it is easy and inexpensive to import up to three pets with you to Mexico, even when traveling on a tourist visa. You can rest assured that it shouldn't be a problem to bring Fido and Fluffy with you. More exotic pets may be a challenge, but you can find all the information in English on my website at www.GrownUpsGuide.com.

The Mexican government requires only a current certificate of good health from your vet, on a template that your vet should have available, issued within 10 days of departure. You'll be required to present proof of current rabies vaccination, and your pet will need to be dewormed by the vet at the time the certificate is issued.

Upon arrival in Mexico, you will be directed to an agricultural extension office at the arrivals terminal where you will present the documents from your vet. An official there will provide a cursory examination of the pet, and off you go! It's that simple.

When I moved to paradise a year ago, I brought my 13-year-old dog Buddy with me on the plane as an Emotional Support Animal at no charge. And a month later, my friend Jackie brought my other dog, Teddy with her when she came to visit.

Most airlines will allow you to bring a single small cat or dog with you on the plane for a $100 charge each way, and they can ride in the cabin with you in a soft sided kennel that fits under the seat.

When I travel to Mexico from the States, I always fly on Southwest Airlines. For some reason Southwest would only allow carryon pets for domestic flights, but not international flights. Since my flight was already booked and paid for, I chose to request a letter from my doctor to bring a pet as an Emotional Support Animal – which was an important learning from my Beta Test. My doctor knew exactly what I needed, and wrote the letter based on a template he already had loaded in his computer.

When reserving the flight online, I simply added in the option to carry an emotional support animal, and I had to present the letter from the doctor at the airport for inspection. That allowed me to not only carry the dog in the cabin, but he could sit on my lap the whole flight, which he did willingly, never budging during the entire trip.

The government has recently made changes to the Emotional Support Animal requirements, and airlines are no longer legally required to honor them like they do professionally trained Service Animals. Check with your airline in advance to makes sure you can pay to carry on your pet, or if they will accept Emotional Support animals in the cabin. You need to reserve early as some airlines limit the number of pets carried in the cabin on any given flight.

And I was impressed that there were pet watering stations in each terminal – equipped with Astroturf and a fake fire hydrant!

And just as importantly, on my Beta Test, I learned that I could get great quality vet care from several different well trained and certified vets locally. There are also outstanding vet clinics in major cities for specialized treatments as well. And like other services in Mexico, veterinary services cost a tiny fraction of what you would pay in the States.

How Will I Handle Banking and Investments?

During my Beta Test, I started out with $500 in cash and an ATM card which I used to get pesos at any of multiple ATM machines. When I signed the lease for my apartment, I was able to show it as proof of local residency and opened a checking account at a local branch of a Mexican bank. That gave me a no-fee ATM and debit card, which I use for all my transactions in Mexico. Plus, I can wire transfer funds directly from my US bank account to my Mexican account and get a much higher exchange rate than using an ATM or debit card.

Until getting a local bank account, you may want to wire yourself money, which can be picked up at a local Electra store, which is a chain of electronics stores owned by a major bank, Azteca, and which "conveniently" offers banking services right in the store, where they hope you will use your newly acquired pesos to buy something.

You can also exchange dollars or withdraw cash using an ATM or credit card at any local bank branch – but you must show your passport to exchange money as a way of trying to control money laundering.

Make friends with the local bank manager or teller and ask about other services your bank can provide. I was amazed to be able to get car insurance right at the bank, and I walked out with my insurance card and a packet of insurance documents in just half an hour.

You should be able to manage all your US or Canadian banking and investments online on your laptop or mobile phone. But you may want to make sure you can make mobile deposits when in Mexico. I can't use mobile banking in Mexico on my Bank of American account, so any checks that I receive physically in Mexico have to be mailed back to a branch in the States. – what a hassle.

Managing your investments is similar, and I keep my IRA in a Principal Securities account, where I can request disbursements by phone or email, and the funds are wired to my US bank account in just a day or two.

I have recently learned that some financial institutions will close your account when they discover you have physically moved overseas. Several people have recently shared their unpleasant stories online in groups I follow, with the happy ending that they were able to get permanent investment support from Charles Schwab International. Make sure you contact your investment company or brokerage to learn about their requirements and ensure you won't have a problem in the future. I will post updated information on my website at www.GrownUpsGuide.com.

How Will I Handle Insurance?

You will also need to deal with insurance issues in planning your escape to paradise. The good news is you will probably end up spending a fraction of what you currently spend on insurance at home.

Home owners Insurance - If you sell your home, you will save hundreds each month on homeowners insurance, and can reduce it to just perhaps $25 to $50 per month of renters insurance, which may include a $1,000,000 liability umbrella plan to cover you against whatever crazy lawsuit or claim someone wants to make against you.

Legal Protection - I also recommend that you get comprehensive legal protection by subscribing to Legal Shield Legal Plan, with a link found at my website. For around $25 a month, you can get free or discounted legal services to protect you or your home business. And for another $16 - $30 a month, you can get proactive ID theft protection for yourself or your whole family.

Auto Insurance - If you sell your car, you will be able to reduce a huge monthly cost. If you decide to live the snowbird lifestyle, you can actually get very inexpensive auto insurance while you are gone through a vacation plan if your car is stored in a garage or otherwise protected. You may also secure insurance that covers you while driving a rented or borrowed car for up to 30 days in the US. Ask your insurance provider about the options.

Medical Care Insurance – This is a major concern we all have, and it is something you should be thinking about in advance to give yourself time to execute it effectively. Traditional **Medicare** will not cover you when you are outside the United States even on vacation, but many Medicare Advantage Plans and private medical insurance plans or Medicare supplement plans may reimburse you for out-of-pocket emergency care expenses overseas. The tricky thing is you can only change your Medicare plan once annually between October and December of each year, so you may want to consider shifting now to a **Medicare Advantage Plans** like AARP Medicare Complete, like I do. It saved me $5,000 annually in premiums, deductibles, and copays before I ever moved overseas, and now it costs me almost nothing. **Medicare Supplement Plans**, and **Private Medical Insurance Plans** may or may not pay for routine or major medical coverage when overseas, so study the options now to choose the best plan and avoid a last-minute rush decision. And when you reach Medicare age of 65, most of your medical insurance costs are covered by either Medicare or Medicare Complete Plans, so you can eliminate most of your medical insurance costs.

Expatriate and Overseas Medical Insurance Plans – US
medical insurance premiums and deductibles are so outrageously high that you may benefit from special medical insurance plans especially created for your overseas life, and which can be incredibly affordable. You may be able to get a plan that covers you out of the country, with a limited time frame in the US, such as 30 days

annually, for as low as $100 per month. There are **Medevac** plans that will evacuate you to a US hospital in the event of a major medical crisis, and there may even be **local private or government medical insurance plans** you can take advantage of as a local resident overseas. And with medical care in Mexico and other countries costing just a tiny fraction of the US cost, you might decide to self-insure most situations, and carry a limited benefit plan that just covers catastrophic medical conditions.

Vision and Dental Insurance Plans may not be needed at all, as medical care is so inexpensive overseas that you can generally pay for all your services in Mexico for what your premium or deductible would be back in the states. I recently had a local ophthalmologist give me a comprehensive eye exam for $35, a computer eye scan ran me $100, and Yag laser surgery to remove scars on my implanted lenses cost just under $300 out of pocket.

Life Insurance – Check your life insurance to update your memory on what is covered and decide what level of coverage you should have. I ended up completely eliminating my life insurance when my only son was grown and well established in his own career, saving me more than $1,500 of premiums per year.

Burial and Cremation Insurance – I purchased a prepaid cremation plan years ago, and it only covers me in the US – not transporting my body to the US. There are some plans that will cover transportation of cremains to the States, which you might want to explore. But with local cremation costs just around $1,000 here in Mexico, it would be more cost effective to choose local cremation and have my ashes sprinkled on the most beautiful beach in the world – at no extra cost!

Your Resource Center - There are so many different insurance needs and options, and the costs, offerings and availability change so frequently, that I have created a whole page of up-to-date information on my website www.GrownUpsGuide.com , so check there for more details.

I'm neither an insurance nor finance professional, and I am providing this overview as a lifestyle coach to help you in your decision-making process when you explore escaping to paradise. You might want to do some preliminary research now to know your options, and then be prepared to execute them with the help of your insurance, financial, or legal advisor when you start to actively implement your move to paradise.

15. READY...SET...GO!

Finally! You've made your decision, and now is the time to pull the trigger to put your plan in action.

A dream is just hope without a plan or a timeline. And once you have made the decision to move to paradise, whether full time or part time, now is the time to start to create your detailed plan and start to put in in action.

You can decide whether you want to announce your intentions to the world or keep it private. I personally think it's great to let everybody know of your upcoming move, because you're going to have people who reach out to help you. That can include friends who offer to help you liquidate your belongings, those who want to buy some of your treasures or furnishings, others willing to adopt a pet you can't take with you, or just friends who will give you emotional support. You can also post your plans on social media, and you may be amazed at the feedback that you get, as well as introductions to people who live in your new destination.

At this point, the clock starts ticking, and you're starting to implement a timeline, whether it's for a month, a year, or five years.

Make Sure You're Ready to Act, And Then Start to Move

I've prepared a Move To Paradise Checklist with all the nitty gritty details to help you plan your move and stay on track. It's available on my website, and it's free of charge. Download it now and start to add dates to all the key milestones you will encounter in the process.

I made the decision to leave the States and move to paradise the first week of July, and exactly two months later, I was on the plane to start my new life, with my dog and three suitcases in tow. It was a stretch, and I worked around the clock to meet my timetable. But I made it happen. And so can you.

It may be more realistic to shoot for a longer time frame, and it's absolutely okay, and it's totally your decision. There is no right or wrong timeline, only the one that works for you.

If you are keeping your home, and just heading out as a snowbird for several months, it's much easier, faster and less complicated than it is to pull up stakes and make a permanent move.

It may take longer if you have a lot of belongings, properties, or responsibilities to deal with. In the same vein, if you're traveling lighter in life and have fewer personal and professional obligations, you may be able to move more quickly. In any event, the last few days and weeks are hectic with last minute details, glitches, unexpected visitors, and just dealing with the detritus of life.

Paul, for example is a Canadian who was looking to move to the tropics somewhere, but hadn't selected a location. He had previously spent several winters in Florida, but decided he wanted a less expensive location where his pension in Canadian dollars would stretch farther. As a result, he was living in a rented room in Ontario, Canada, to be close to his son and grandson, while searching for his dream location. He joined a coaching program where he heard a lot about Isla Mujeres, and it sounded exactly like what he was looking for. He decided to hop on a plane and see what everyone was talking about. He spent one month on the island for a Beta Test and decided to make the move. He headed back to Canada at the end of the month and spent the next two months wrapping up all his loose ends. He changed phone services, renewed his driver's license, set up new banking arrangements, got medical exams, and refilled his prescription medications for six months. He visited with his six siblings and several good friends and went to the cemetery to put flowers on his mother's grave. He sifted through all his belongings, packing two large suitcases with the clothes and the few belongings that he wanted to take with him. He donated everything else to charity, including his car, rather than hassle with trying to sell it. He spent as much time as he could with his two grandchildren and his son. And exactly two months later, he headed back to Mexico to set up his new life in paradise.

It really can be that simple, depending on where you are in your life, and which lifestyle option you choose.

Celebrating Your Life Change with Family and Friends

This may be the perfect time to see family members and friends whom you've not connected with in a while. Having a farewell party adds finality to your decision, and lets your family and friends celebrate this important next step in your life.

As I prepared to move, I planned a mini family reunion, and my brother and his wife drove to Texas from Florida, my son and his wife flew in from Oregon, and my cousin Debbie drove down from Austin to San Antonio with her two kids for a final get together before I flew to Mexico. We spent hours in the living room going through photo albums, scrap books, hand crocheted afghans and my grandmother's recipe books written in longhand, college diplomas and dad's business and Masonic memorabilia and other family heirlooms. We distributed them among each family group, earmarking special photos and mementos to each of the extended family members. My son and his wife took home photo albums, scrapbooks, and long-hidden treasures that his wife had never seen. I gave them special Christmas ornaments to remember festive family events.

My cousin Debbie selected items for her two siblings, and we distributed photos and keepsakes among all family members. And it was fun! Her family had moved from Minnesota to Las Vegas when the three kids were small, so she and her siblings were never able to share in all the family reunions, weddings, funerals and the like. Her dad died when she was in high school, further separating her and her two brothers from the rest of the family that stayed in Minnesota. During the farewell process, we discovered a video of her parents' wedding which no one in her family had ever seen! She was so thrilled and shared it with her siblings to everyone's great joy.

For my imminent move, we wrapped several events together into a festive long weekend. We booked a patio at a local Mexican restaurant (of course), and celebrated my mom's 97th birthday, with many family and friends aware that it would probably be the last time we would see her. We celebrated my departure with great Mexican food and lots of margaritas, dozens of photos, and posted live videos of the festivities on Facebook. I bought a box full of small mementos from my home, and we drew names so each person could take home a special treasure they had previously admired during visits. This provided closure and the opportunity to celebrate my new adventure, and to socialize with friends that I knew I wouldn't see for a while.

If you plan a similar celebration, make sure you plan it for a few weeks before your departure, so you're not so harried with all the last-minute details.

Regardless of whether you are planning your move for a month or a year away, the final weeks are hectic with last minute details, glitches, unexpected visitors, and just dealing with the flotsam of life. There are so many tiny details that need to be attended to, and things always pop up at the last minute.

Don't let all those bothersome details distract you from the big picture. You are moving to paradise, and this is just part of the process. In a few days or weeks, you will be living the life of your dreams. Soldier through all the last-minute glitches and headaches and keep focused on your goal. Because a month after you move, all the worries, frazzled nerves, irritating challenges, and the trauma of letting go of so much will all fade away, and it won't matter at all in your new life in paradise.

16. LEARN THE NEW LANGUAGE

You may be considering moving to a country where English is spoken, like Belize, the Bahamas, The Virgin Islands, or farther away like Australia, New Zealand, England or Ireland. If so, you won't have to deal with learning a new language. But if your plan is to move to a country with a different official language, you will definitely benefit from learning the language as fast and as well as possible.

The ability to speak the native language wherever you move will play a vital role in not just helping you assimilate into your new home, but will also help you to easily navigate life in your new country. It will also make your experiences living in paradise much richer and more satisfying, allowing you to communicate directly with others, explain yourself well, and participate in events with local residents that you might never otherwise experience.

Among my friends here in paradise, learning Spanish is a top priority, and many are taking online classes or working with a tutor to improve their skills. They know how much mastering the language can contribute to their enjoyment of their new home. And I can guarantee you, as a fluent Spanish speaker, that you will also be thankful when you feel comfortable communicating in the native language. It will open doors, unlock new experiences, connect you with people, and simplify your life.

It's Easier Today Than Ever Before

Fortunately for most of us, Spanish is perhaps the easiest language to learn, and many Americans have some kind of experience with Spanish language classes in high school or college. Other romance languages like Portuguese, French and Italian are also fairly easy to learn.

Imagine trying to learn Greek, Russian, Chinese, Japanese, or Thai. I can't fathom the difficulty of trying to learn a language with a different alphabet, or where you read right to left!

The world's most populous languages are Mandarin Chinese and Hindi, followed by Spanish and English. In fact, there are more native Spanish speakers in the world, 350 million, than native English speakers at 340 million. All other popular languages that you might have studied fall far down the list: there are 203 million native Portuguese speakers, 101 million German speakers, 67 million French speakers, and 61 million Italian speakers.

Therefore, if you choose to study Spanish, you will find many uses of the language, scores of different training programs, and lots of ways to engage in the language by watching different Spanish language TV channels in the US and Canada, including Univision, Telemundo, and TV Azteca.

In the past it was expensive to learn a foreign language, as I did in college, and later when I went through a Berlitz intensive conversational Portuguese training program prior to my husband's transfer to Brazil. His company paid more than $3,000 for daily in-person lessons for two months, and I had to drive into an office and meet with a teacher face to face 5 days a week.

The good news is that learning to speak a foreign language today is easy, inexpensive, and available on demand through your phone or laptop.

As soon as you know where you plan to move, start learning the language. Study for at least a few minutes every day and listen to cartoons and children's programs on TV or YouTube to learn like children do. When you do actually move to paradise, speaking the language will allow you to hit the ground faster and smoother than you imagine, and it will open up so many doors to new people and experiences in life.

If language lessons are part of your runaway plan, visit my website for information on different programs to help you master the local language long before you start packing your bags for paradise.

17. YOU'RE ON YOUR WAY!

B elieve it or not, by this point you are more than halfway there. You've found your paradise and have made the decision to grab the gold ring of happiness. Everything else becomes details, bothersome but necessary distractions along the road to happiness.

Getting There

As you embark on your journey to paradise, you will figure out how you will actually travel there, generally by plane, or by car to many locations in Mexico. Some people travel by boat or even motorcycles, and they are free spirts who are marching to their own drummer and probably don't need my help.

You will need your passport of course, and hopefully your residency visa stamped into your passport, for yourself and all your family members. And you will need your travel documents for the pets as well.

Make sure you bring lots of small denomination bills to use along the way, and keep at least $100 in small bills in your safe in your new location for your next trip back home.

And you will want a place to stay for a few days until you find your perfect home, so you many want to book several days in an affordable hotel to give you chance to find just the right place for you – for now.

Arriving in Paradise

When you arrive in paradise, you will want to either move into your pre-selected home or look for the right home based on new availabilities and hopefully off-season rock-bottom low rental prices.

You will have fun adding to the furnishings and personalizing it so it becomes your home, not just a house.

You will want to arrange temporary transportation – no need to rush a big decision like buying a car during your first days. You can rent a car at incredibly low rates, or rent a fun golf cart, or just walk and take taxis like you did on your Beta Test.

You may want to open a bank account or check in with your already-selected banker to update your address and withdraw or exchange currency.

Fitting In and Building Community

You will be connecting with people you met during your Beta Test and tuning into the local vibe and catching up to speed with what is happening locally.

Make sure you get out and meet new people every day and set time to grab a bite or a drink with the people you met on your Beta Test or chatted with online while preparing your move.

Now's the time to volunteer for a charity to get involved with the local community, and to add structure and purpose to your life.

And you can explore your local market, take adventure trips to nearby towns and cities, climb pyramids or explore hidden lakes or ancient ruins.

Relax! You have made it to paradise!

Yes, there is a lot more to do to implement your move to paradise. But don't let all those details derail your plan to run away from home or distract you from your vision of joy in paradise.

I'm writing a whole second book to hold your hand and walk you step-by-step through the process from the point when you make your decision to move to paradise, until you get happily set up and living the life of your dreams.

It's called **The Runaway Roadmap: Your Step-By-Step Guide to Escape to Paradise and Live Richly on Any Budget**. It's available online on Amazon in the Kindle store, and on my website www.TheGrownUpsGuide.com . It will be available in a paperback, eBook, and audio book format, and you can also get a workbook to help you plan all the nitty gritty details.

But don't buy it before you are ready to implement your move to paradise.

Right now, you have all the information you need to start down the path of discovery that will lead you to your joyous vision of the future, to identify and research your dream home, and to test the waters to make sure it is right for you.

Do your research. Vacation with a purpose. Do your Beta Test. If it's not right, keep researching and vacationing and conducting Beta Tests until you find just the right place for you.

That will give you the certainty and confidence to take the bold decision to move to paradise – and to choose whichever type of lifestyle feels right to you. Only then should you focus on implementing all the bothersome details and sometimes big challenges you will need to address to make your dream come true.

First make your decision, then your plan. And when you have those two done, you hold in your hand the keys to your happiness.

Remember, keep your eye on your goal. You are working towards joy, peace, satisfaction, freedom, stimulation, and contentment. You deserve them. Claim them for yourself, as your birthright, and don't let anything hold you back.

18. WHICH PATH WILL YOU CHOOSE FROM HERE?

───────

In 1912, American Poet Robert Frost wrote a poem called "The Road Not Taken." Today it's considered to be the best-known American poem of the 20th century, and perhaps the best-known American poem, period. You probably remember it from your high school English class.

And it's as relevant today as it was more than a century ago.

The Road Not Taken – By Robert Frost

Two roads diverged in a yellow wood,
And sorry I could not travel both
And be one traveler, long I stood
And looked down one as far as I could
To where it bent in the undergrowth;

Then took the other, as just as fair,
And having perhaps the better claim,
Because it was grassy and wanted wear;
Though as for that the passing there
Had worn them really about the same,

And both that morning equally lay
In leaves no step had trodden black.
Oh, I kept the first for another day!
Yet knowing how way leads on to way,
I doubted if I should ever come back.

I shall be telling this with a sigh
Somewhere ages and ages hence:

**Two roads diverged in a wood, and I—
I took the one less traveled by,
And that has made all the difference.**

Today, more than 100 years later, you face the same choice. Which path will you take?

The one you know and feel comfortable with, or the one less traveled?

The fact is that you will never know what will happen on the path you don't take.

It's also important to remember that you don't have to stay on the path you choose forever. It's a choice you make for today, each and every day for the rest of your life.

And when it's no longer a choice you are happy with, you can make a new choice to do something different or go someplace else.

Whatever you choose, I hope you find your magical place that makes your heart sing.

19. THE CHANCE TO CREATE YOUR HAPPY ENDING

Fortunately, there are many happy endings in paradise.

But they START with you.

You've got to choose to be happy. No one can make you happy except for you.

And you have the option to make choices and take actions to live the life you choose. Deciding not to act now is also a choice, and it's a perfectly valid choice.

You can decide that running away from home is too risky, too scary, too far away, too difficult, too lonely, or just not what you want at this point in your life.

And that's perfectly fine. You are taking responsibility for your own life choices.

But after reading this book, you now have all the information you need to make an informed decision to embark on a new life in paradise – or not.

And it's never too late. Each day you can make new choices which will take you on the next journey of adventure and discovery.

Because you never know who you will meet and where you will go when you decide to run away from home and move to paradise.

20. MY HAPPILY EVER AFTER

I moved to paradise almost two years ago, and never looked back. I have enjoyed every day, meeting new people, savoring new adventures, discovering new places, connecting with so many wonderful people, and exploring the amazing culture and history.

Every day has filled my heart with joy and happiness. I have been more content than I had been in decades. Moving to paradise was definitely the right choice for me.

Whenever anyone asked me how long I planned to live here, I always replied, "Until I don't want to be here anymore." That's because my life is in my control, and I can choose to live where I want, how I want, and do what I want with my time, talents and energy.

The decision to move to paradise, this particular place that I now call home, is my decision for today. It doesn't have to be forever, just for now. And when it's not right for me anymore, I can make another decision about what I want to do with my life.

And so can you.

The freedom to make life decisions with confidence and with joy is an amazing, life changing gift. And right now, you have the power to make those decisions with your life, like I have with mine.

And the story is never completely over.

Nine months ago, while I was actively researching and writing this book, I opened my door to meet Paul, a colleague in a coaching program. He had just arrived in Isla in the aftermath of a small hurricane, which caused his apartment to not be ready to move into upon his arrival as planned. He was coming to Isla for his first vacation with a purpose. It wasn't even a Beta Test, rather a spontaneous decision to hop on a plane and check out this place we were all talking about. And as a colleague in our joint coaching program, I of course opened my home to help him when he arrived and had no place to stay because of the hurricane shutdown.

30 days and three hurricanes later, my life changed once again.

While I was contentedly enjoying my life in paradise, the universe gifted me with another blessing. My soul mate Paul was delivered to my front door, suitcases in hand, and I was in the right place, the right time, and the right state of mind to receive that amazing gift of love.

Now we have embarked on a new adventure in paradise, as a couple, looking forward to new experiences, learnings, challenges, and opportunities.

I moved to paradise looking for peace and happiness. And as a bonus, I have found love and joy.

Wherever you go on your journey, I hope you find the same.

# # #

MEET THE AUTHOR

D iane Huth is the Runaway Sherpa and will guide you on your life of transformation as you run away from home and escape to paradise.

After a wonderful 30-year career in corporate marketing, she became unemployable due to her age, and faced a life of limited possibilities surviving on Social Security in the States as she cared for her elderly mother with dementia.

By extensive research, exploration, relentless questions, and vacations with a purpose, she successfully left behind her Texas life to move to the white sandy beaches of Isla Mujeres, which means The Island of Women, just 7 miles off the coast of Cancun in sun-kissed Mexico.

She ran away from a dreary dead-end existence in the States to create a vibrant joy-filled life replete with many warm friendships, meaningful activities that engage her time and talents, a thriving business as a career coach, author and marketing consultant, and daily gratitude for being as close to heaven as possible while on this earth.

She lives in a charming second-floor home with an amazing rooftop terrace which overlooks both the Bay of Cancun to the west, and the deep turquoise water of the Caribbean Sea to the East, just 90 miles away from western Cuba. She shares her home with her 12-year-old blind schnauzer-terrier mutt Teddy the Wonderdog, and five island kitties who have chosen to live in her home, and enter and leave at will through wide open doors on the balcony and the picture windows facing the blazing sunset to the west.

And she was recently blessed by the arrival of Paul, her new life partner, who she says was a gift from Ixchel, the Mayan goddess of love, health, fertility, abundance, medicine, and rainbows!

Diane is the Amazon best-selling author of two career guides, and runs a busy career coaching business helping job seekers find their dream jobs at www.DianeHuth.com and www.BrandYouGuide.com .

And she is now launching her Escape To Paradise runaway coaching, to help freedom-seekers like you to reinvent your life discover just how easy and affordable it is to create a joy-filled life in paradise — wherever you find your paradise to be.

Reach out to Diane at any of her websites or social media pages:

www.GrownUpsGuide.com — website with dozens of free bonuses and valuable resources

www.EscapeToParadiseToday.com — training, coaching and mentoring programs to help you on your way to paradise

www.Facebook.com/TheGrownUpsGuideToRunningAwayFromHome - enjoy this Facebook page with scores of live videos giving you a bird's-eye view into everyday life in paradise

www.Facebook.com/groups/EscapeToParadiseToday - Diane's mentoring and training group to engage closely to coach you on your journey to paradise

You can also reach Diane by email at Diane@DianeHuth.com

She'd love to hear from you, and learn of your own experience in running away from home and escaping to paradise.

BEFORE YOU GO

It means the world to me that you bought my book.

Providing inspiration to people is my passion and I look forward to YOUR feedback.

So if you liked this book, I'd like to ask for a small favor. Would you be so kind as to leave an honest review on Amazon? Even just a sentence or two will be immensely appreciated.

And if you loved the book, I'd be thrilled if you give me a 5-star rating!

Click Here to leave a review - I really appreciate it!

From your friend, mentor and escape to paradise coach and supporter,

Diane Huth,

The Runaway Sherpa

5 Star Review!